the
Other
Mind's
Eye

The Gateway
To The Hidden Treasures
Of Your Mind

Allen C. Sargent

Cover design and illustration: Sandy Novak & Tom Tuttle

First Printing September 1999

Printed in the United States of America by
Bertelsmann Industry Services

ISBN 0-9674831-0-7

12 11 10 9 8 7 6 5 4 3 2

Foreword

We live in a world that is constantly changing and evolving. In order to cope effectively, the pace of our ability to learn and think must keep up with the advances in our physical technology. This requires the development of practical skills and tools which help us to more efficiently achieve goals and address challenges in our personal and professional lives.

For the past twenty-five years, the techniques and methods of NLP have provided many powerful means to create a better future for ourselves, our families and our professional colleagues. Among its many areas of application, NLP has been used to attain personal goals, resolve emotional issues, enhance learning and creativity, increase physical and mental health, and improve business.

Al Sargent's discoveries with respect to Internal Dominant Eye Accessing represents one of the most intriguing and significant developments in NLP in the past decade. These discoveries, presented in *The Other Mind's Eye*, demonstrate both creativity and the attention to detail which are the hallmarks of all important innovations.

The tools and methods covered in the book represent the best that NLP has to offer: they are simple, quick, grounded in experience, but also theoretically sound. And most important, they are both effective and ecological in producing meaningful change; and may be applied as an adjunct to existing NLP processes.

The Other Mind's Eye offers practical and simple step-by-step procedures with which to improve memory, deal with stuck states, solve problems and develop better awareness of and control over your own thinking process. It is clear that these procedures have been empirically tested and refined as the result of extensive practical applications.

Following the interactive flow of a seminar experience, the ideas and procedures presented by Al and Marilyn draw out our natural intuitions, and then introduce us to surprising discoveries which open the doorway to new possibilities that we have not yet considered.

I wish to express my sincere congratulations to both Al and Marilyn Sargent for this innovative and practical NLP book. I am confident that this book will contribute to further growth of NLP and help people to improve their lives in many ways.

Robert B. Dilts
Santa Cruz, California
July, 1999

"A theory is the more impressive the greater the simplicity of its premises is, the more different kinds of things it relates, and the more extended its area of applicability."

Albert Einstein

Acknowledgements

Someone once said, "You can accomplish anything, you just can't accomplish it alone." I like to believe this statement refers to the fact that we are all in the world together, and that without working together very little can be accomplished.

All information available to the world is stacked upon the learnings that came before. The information contained in this book represents the efforts of all those who questioned, then discovered, and then shared what they had learned.

I recognize that that I have not been on this journey alone, and I am grateful to my many friends and colleagues who have supported me throughout the development of this new technology.

Thank You

Table of Contents

Introduction

The structure and applications of Internal Dominant Eye Accessing form the basis of the tools that allow us to begin to answer the question "Why" as it applies to understanding how we code and respond to emotional information. This new technology gives us the structure to develop habits and personal strategies that lead to having more of the good things we want in our lives.

Neuro-Linguistic Programming (NLP) is the study of human excellence. It asks the question, "What works, and how can it work even better?" By analyzing (modeling) the specific behaviors and internal thinking processes (strategies) of individuals who consistently demonstrate excellence in their field, those strategies can be identified down to very fine details. Once this has been accomplished, those strategies can be used by others to accomplish the same level of excellence. The same concept holds true for professional goals, interpersonal relationships, and a person's self-esteem.

Behaviors are relatively easy to identify. The exciting and challenging task is to precisely elicit internal thinking processes, beliefs, and motivations. This task becomes even more challenging because very often, those who are top performers are not consciously aware of their internal thinking patterns that lead to their success.

In the early 1970's, Richard Bandler, John Grinder, Robert Dilts, Judith Delozier, Leslie Cameron-Bandler and others discovered ways to access and identify specific and reliable templates that elicit internal mental processes, language patterns, and behavioral characteristics of successful people. This was the beginning of Neuro-

Linguistic Programming. Neuro represents the internal workings of the brain, Linguistic refers to how language influences our experience both internally and in communication with others, and Programming is how to install effective strategies into our own life.

The modeling templates identified in NLP offer a structure to analyze all aspects of any system, including the system that is within all individuals at a personal level, all the way up to and including global politics, and health.

As with any field of technology, NLP has specific terminology to represent concepts and principles of interest to the field. Throughout this book, much of the "jargon" used in the field of NLP has either been translated into user-friendly language, or explained as it is presented. It is my belief that anyone with an interest in "What is possible?" will benefit by reading this book, and using the valuable information within it.

I would like to take this opportunity to introduce my wife Marilyn Sargent. The format of this book is as an interactive exchange with participants in a seminar on Internal Dominant Eye Accessing that Marilyn and I present together.

Marilyn has an extensive background in NLP and has a private consulting practice in the Los Angeles area. She has been a part of the discoveries discussed in this book from the very beginning and, more often than not, she has been the test subject throughout the developmental stages.

Preface

Young Johnny is walking home from school when a car drives by and one of the teenage occupants of the car throws a water balloon that hits Johnny on his left leg. Instantly, two separate impressions are simultaneously imprinted into Johnny's memory, one in the left hemisphere of his brain which is responsible for logical linear thinking, and another in his right hemisphere which is more interested in the processing of spatial relationship.

These two related yet separate perceptions of the same event are emotionally coded according to the specific qualities and interests of each hemisphere of the brain. In the left hemisphere of Johnny's brain the information may be coded as a simple case of three teenagers who were bored and wanted to have some fun. With this understanding, Johnny is most likely going to continue on his way home, change into some dry clothing, get a snack, maybe do his homework, and go to a friend's house to play. Having this perception of the event, it is unlikely that Johnny will be affected in a way that is more than an inconvenience.

In Johnny's right hemisphere, however, the same event could have a more far-reaching effect on him. His right hemisphere is more concerned with how he is personally involved in the situation and how it may affect his safety. His right hemisphere might perceive this event more like the following. Three big teenagers out to cause trouble drove by, selected him to terrorize, and threw something at him from a car. Next they drove off laughing at his misfortune, probably circling the block to get yet another shot at him.

With this perception, Johnny races home, runs upstairs, and finds refuge in his room as the effects of the stress response fade and his body starts to return to normal. Not only has he lost his appetite for an after school snack, but also he is in no mood to do his homework. Even the possibility of going to his friend's house to play is out of the question, because the teenagers might spot him, and this time he might not escape so luckily.

How Johnny actually responds to a situation similar to this one will generally be somewhere between the examples I have given, since the left and right hemispheres of the brain communicate information back and forth through a network of fibers in the brain called the *corpus callosum*. Information stored in Johnny's brain from previous experiences will also have an important influence on his response to this event.

Since the most primary and vital functions of the brain involve survival and personal safety issues, the brain automatically responds to and evaluates events that might threaten a person's immediate safety. In most people, the right hemisphere of the brain stores emotionally charged memories, while at the same time, the left hemisphere records a relatively unemotional sequence of events. There are two separate and unique pictorial representations for each event in our lives for which an external visual stimulus has been imprinted.

Think of how often we have heard the phrase "I see it in my mind's eye." Imagine how many possibilities will be opened up by understanding your "other mind's eye." When we recall an event with the right hemisphere's "mind's eye" our response will be very different than if we recall it with the left hemisphere's "mind's eye." Each hemisphere of the brain records and recalls useful information. If we consistently utilize the perceptions from only one side of our brain, our choices are limited, often leaving personal issues unresolved. "I have half a mind to…" is another phrase we often hear people use. If this is descriptive of what is actually happening in our thinking process, we may literally be using only half of our potential.

Learning how to have conscious control of which hemispheric image to utilize broadens the range of choices and responses available to us. Additional benefits result from being able to integrate information from both hemispheres when dealing with an issue.

This book is based on an edited transcript of a two-day seminar given in 1997. Some examples have been added in the process of editing. In this book you will learn how your brain codes information for emotional responses, and how to consciously access information stored in both hemispheres. You will also learn simple step-by-step techniques to help you use your entire brain to get what you want in life. The participants (whose names were changed to respect their privacy) offered valuable insights, and asked some very interesting questions. I believe their questions will help to answer questions you may have as you read this book.

Allen C. Sargent

Note to reader:

To facilitate the smoothness of reading, "he," "she," "his," and "her" are used to connote a singular pronoun, not as a gender distinction.

Discovering "The Other Mind's Eye"

As with all new discoveries, "Internal Dominant Eye Accessing™" is the culmination of information from a variety of sources. In this section, I will give a brief history of the specific pieces of information leading to the discovery of Internal Dominant Eye Accessing, which then led to the formation of "The Hemispheric Eye Model™" (also referred to as "THE Model™").

One of the major tools used for personal change is visualization. Throughout my life, I had a difficult time consciously accessing internal images. Seemingly simple tasks, such as trying to make internal images bigger or brighter, did not have much effect on my internal experiences.

Many of us who might be considered "mind's eye challenged" stand almost in disbelief as those who are "mind's eye gifted" change and manipulate their internal pictures with ease. I have a friend who gets such vivid pictures in her mind's eye that she almost has to walk around them. Visualization comes so easily for her that she can't avoid getting pictures.

After about two years of pretending "as if" I were getting pictures, it finally occurred to me that it might be the *way* I was trying to access pictures internally that was making the difference.

NLP models the structure of excellence by finding the component pieces that are an integral part of a successful strategy. Since I recognized the value in being able to access internal images, I began to find out all I could about *how* those who are "visually gifted" were accessing their internal pictures. My quest for more visual access led to the discovery of Internal Dominant Eye Accessing.

Even people such as myself, who could have been considered "mind's eye challenged," remember dreaming, at least to some extent. Dreaming indicates that some part of the brain is capable of visualizing something that is not actually in our conscious reality. Knowing that many people believe that dreaming involves having access to the right hemisphere, I began to wonder if those who could easily visualize in a conscious state of awareness somehow had more access to their right hemisphere when they were awake than those who had difficulty visualizing. I thought that if I could find out how those who were visually gifted were visualizing, I might be able to have some conscious control of my own internal images.

Besides a desire to have better access to visualization, there were four main pieces that led to the discovery of Internal Dominant Eye Accessing.

The first piece came many years ago when I was a golf professional. Jack Nicklaus had discussed seeing the golf ball dominantly with his right eye before he started his backswing. Since he tilted his head slightly during his backswing, it was evident to him that he could not actually see the ball with his right eye any longer, because his nose was now between his right eye and the ball. Since he could still see the ball from this position, he had somehow switched so that he was seeing the ball with his left eye. The important thing I learned from this was that even though we do see out of both eyes, we see out of either the left or right eye more dominantly at any given moment in time.

The second piece of information came during a workshop I attended on accelerated learning. In the workshop they discussed how information is received into both the left and right hemispheres from what we see, hear, and feel. The goal for accelerated learning is to input information into all sensory channels in each hemisphere. Recall of the information can then be accessed in either hemisphere through each sensory channel. We will discuss this process in more detail a little bit later. (Chapter 3 - *Understanding Hemispheric Dominance*)

The third piece I learned at a lecture about Ericksonian Hypnosis. This piece had to do with a naturally occurring shift of hemispheric dominance from the left hemisphere of the brain to the right hemisphere, and then back to the left hemisphere, approximately every ninety minutes. This shift happens out of our conscious awareness and varies slightly among individuals. The naturally occurring shift of hemispheric dominance is known as *ultradian rhythms*, and, since it plays an important role in how we store and recall information, we will be covering it in more detail later. (Chapter 4 - *Natural Shifts in Hemispheric Dominance*)

The fourth piece came when I had an opportunity to talk with an ophthalmologist about eye dominance, and he demonstrated how to determine which eye is currently dominant (externally). Later, we will demonstrate how to do this, and how it is a valuable tool in learning to access your internal dominant eye. (Chapter 6 – *How to Determine Eye Dominance*)

Knowing that we can identify our external dominant eye, I began to wonder if the same thing was happening internally. I had often been told to "see with my mind's eye." **What I discovered is that we actually have two "mind's eyes." We have one image coded dominantly in the left hemisphere of the brain, and another separate image coded dominantly in the right hemisphere of the brain.**

In essence, we have two separate pictures and two separate perceptions for each event in our life. They may be similar in many ways, and yet they are different. Which image we are accessing will have a very important impact on how we perceive the world, what we feel our choices are, and how we go about responding to these choices.

The Internal Dominant Eye Accessing processes are simple and easy to use with yourself and with others. To understand the processes well, it is important to have a basic understanding of what is going on inside your brain. One of my favorite quotes comes from a biologist named Lyle Watson, who said, **"If the brain were so simple that we could understand it, we would be so simple that we couldn't."** With this in mind, we are going to keep this explanation as simple as it needs to be, and still have enough information to understand how our brains process incoming visual information. There is a great deal of value in understanding how external information influences our perceptual filters. We will be giving you enough information about how Internal Dominant Eye Accessing works for you to be confident using the processes with yourself and with others. After we have explained the more detailed concepts, you will be able to *experience* the value of having conscious access to your "other mind's eye."

How Perceptions Are Formed

In NLP terminology the word *modality* refers to our senses. *Visual* is what we see, *auditory* is what we hear, and *kinesthetic* refers to our feelings. In much of the literature in NLP, the sense of smell (*olfactory*) and the sense of taste (*gustatory*) are grouped with the kinesthetics, although these modalities may be identified separately. In the more specific category of kinesthetics, there are three distinctions of feelings. One involves *tactile* sensations, which has to do with our sense of touch and temperature. The second is called *proprioceptive* and relates to our visceral feelings and body movement. The third part of our kinesthetics we call our *emotions,* such as happy, sad, worried, and excited. **Emotions are our composite evaluations and perceptions from what we see, hear, and feel both internally and externally**

I mentioned earlier that I had attended a seminar on accelerated learning. In the seminar, I learned that both hemispheres are receiving input in all of the modalities.

(See chart A)

Hemispheric Specialization of the Brain

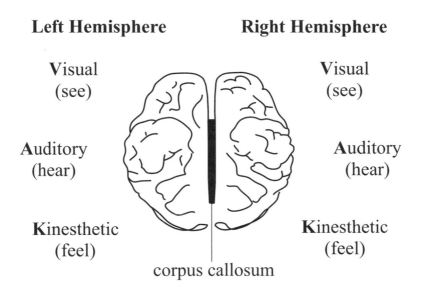

Left Hemisphere　　　　**Right Hemisphere**

Visual
(see)

Auditory
(hear)

Kinesthetic
(feel)

Visual
(see)

Auditory
(hear)

Kinesthetic
(feel)

corpus callosum

We feel in one world and think and give names in another.

Left Hemisphere	Right Hemisphere
Logical	Spatial Information
Linear	Metaphors
Analytical	Sense of Identity
Data	Emotionally Charged Memories
Facts	Total Picture Perceptions
Speech Center	Poetic Language
Familiar Information	Unfamiliar Information

Each hemisphere has an independent capacity for visual, auditory, and kinesthetic processing. Beliefs, strategies, and overall perceptions are unique to the cognitive style of each hemisphere.

CHART A

The brain is divided into two hemispheres, both with unique, special functions and abilities.

For most people, the left hemisphere specializes in logical, linear information, such as facts and data. Most of the speech centers are located in the left hemisphere. This is what I refer to as the checkbook world where scheduling, speech, and technical analysis take place.

The right hemisphere is more concerned with spatial thoughts and relationships. This is where our identity and how we relate in the world seem to live. The right hemisphere is also where metaphor is processed. We use metaphor to introduce new perceptions, to update limiting beliefs, and to introduce new behavioral options. There is a speech center in the right hemisphere that is responsible for putting the language from the left hemisphere into meaningful phrases. It is the right hemisphere that has the ability to distinguish the meaning of a word or statement from the tonality of the speaker. For example, "darkroom," used to develop film, or "dark room," describing a room without light, is easy to distinguish in normal conversation. The right hemisphere is also where emotionally charged memories are stored. If an event is very emotional, chances are it can be accessed in the right hemisphere.

The two hemispheres of the brain communicate with each other by sharing information through a network of fibers called the corpus callosum. The corpus callosum unites the specialties of each hemisphere into a perception that combines the logical, technical skills of the left hemisphere with the relationship and identity focus from the right hemisphere. The transfer and sharing of information between the hemispheres creates our experience from what we refer to as one brain, even though the information comes from the two hemispheres, each with its own cognitive style.

Years ago, research scientists tested the electrical activity in the brains of patients who had seizures. A seizure is caused by massive random firing of the neurons in the brain. Scientists found that a seizure would often start in one hemisphere and then transfer over to the other hemisphere. As a last resort, researchers severed the corpus callosum to keep the firing from jumping over to the other hemisphere. When they did this, it kept the hemispheres from communicating with each other, a condition referred to as *split brain*.

Researchers discovered that each side of the brain had its own sense of awareness, memory, and cognitive thinking. Each hemisphere had all the functional aspects that are normally considered to be whole brain functions. Patients with a split brain condition could still learn and later recall new information, even without the advantage of having the two hemispheres directly communicating with each other. This is not to say that split brain patients had the same flowing integrated aspects of whole-brain thinking, but it does give evidence of the unique perceptual potential of each hemisphere.

It is important for our purposes here to note that each side of the brain does have potential for its own thoughts, memories and perceptions based on its special interests and cognitive style.

Next, I want to explain how we form perceptions from visual input. When we see something externally a certain physical sequence begins.

(See Chart B)

Visual Pathways

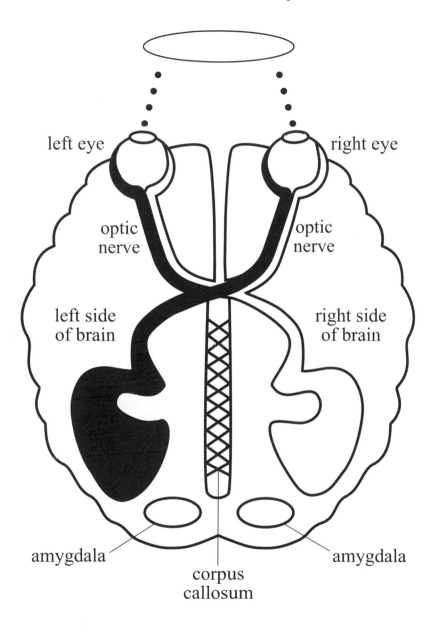

CHART B

To begin with, we will focus on the retina of the eye where cones and rods take information in and send it to the brain. The eyes can be thought of as being separated vertically into equal halves. Information coming into the eye from the outside of our visual field connects to the retina and enters into an area just behind the eyeballs called the *optic chiasm*. The information is then transferred into the receiving eye side of the brain. Information received into the inside, or nasal side, of our visual field connects to the retina and travels into the optic chiasm and is then transferred into the hemisphere opposite from the eye that is receiving the input.

Essentially, each eye is taking in information that goes to both sides of the brain. **If somebody has the use of only one eye, they are still getting information into both hemispheres.** Once the image gets to the brain, it is transferred along optic fibers to the visual cortex area of the brain to a group of cells. These cells are the analyzers. They analyze the input sent from the cones and rods of the pupil.

The analyzer cells are surrounded by another group of cells that organize the information into meaningful pictures. Then a third group of cells coordinates the input from the "see" and "hear" into a single perception. At this point, overall evaluation and emotions are created. At the same time this process is happening in the left hemisphere, it is also happening simultaneously in the right hemisphere.

An evaluation is going to be formed based on the hemispheric function or cognitive style for each side of the brain. Information processed in my left hemisphere is going to have a logical, linear evaluation. The information that comes into the right hemisphere is going to be processed with attention toward spatial relationship and identity.

Therefore, in our memory, we actually have two complete and separate perceptions from the images of any event.

There is a small almond-shaped part of the brain called the *amygdala*. During the formative years of childhood, the amygdala is responsible for taking input from an external sensory stimulus and evaluating what it means emotionally. The amygdala is also the part of the brain that is responsible for responding to a similar external stimulus in the future. Since there is an amygdala in each hemisphere of the brain, whatever we see out in our environment is put into the brain in both hemispheres with the potential of each hemisphere having its own separate emotional evaluation.

When I see a picture in my mind's eye, or in reality, of a tall man with a green shirt, there is going to be an emotional evaluation of it. Depending on the specific circumstances at the time of the original imprint, the emotional evaluation might be something very good with a warm cozy feeling, or it may be something that serves as a warning of impending danger, or even something perceived as neutral.

In summary, we have two hemispheres and two separate concepts, resulting in two separate and unique perceptions of each event in our lives. This applies to past, current, and future events. The difference in the cognitive perceptions from each hemisphere varies depending on the intensity of the event.

(Note to reader: This book is based on the transcripts from a two day seminar. From this point on, A: indicates Al, M: indicates Marilyn, and participants names are in *italics.)*

A: Does anyone have any questions up to this point?

Tim: So you are analyzing, organizing, and coordinating. Is that a linear reduction?

A: Yes.

Tim: Is it that reduction process that helps create our experiences from visual and auditory input?

M: Right, it's how we make meaning out of the external world.

A: What we see, what we hear, and what we feel, creates what we call, in NLP terms, a *meta-k* (beyond or about a feeling). The meta-k, or evaluation, can be interpreted as either a positive or negative experience. What we see, hear, feel, smell, and taste, as well as our internal beliefs about who we are in the world, dictates our emotional equivalence from external input.

We can be happy or we can be scared, in response to similar circumstances, depending on our internal programming, which is based on earlier events and perceptions from our personal history file. The linear, left hemisphere of the brain may have a different interpretation of the meaning of an event or an imprint than the right hemisphere has for the same event.

Emotionally charged material is more likely going to be in the right hemisphere, whereas the left hemisphere is going to be more concerned with logic and facts. So to answer your question, the evaluation is going to be different, even though the process is the same, in each hemisphere.

Tim: Is that a linear sequence, or is that happening all at once?

A: It is linear, and it is very quick. The amygdala responds to an external stimulus, and the emotional evaluation is prior to conscious thought, which happens somewhere else in the limbic system (a complex set of structures in the brain responsible for emotions). We respond emotionally before we become conscious of what is triggering the emotion.

M: Which is what happens with the imprinting of old beliefs. As a child we are imprinted with beliefs about ourselves, and the world in general, based on a particular event. Then as an adult we might hear a loud noise, and we are terrified. We don't know why we are terrified, we just react and respond because the brain gives the evaluation before the thought is even conscious.

Tim: The other part of the question was, as the retina receives the light to a certain portion of the retina, there is a certain amount of deletion at that point. In this linear process does that deletion process continue?

A: The amount of information received by the optic nerve is about $1/200^{th}$ of what is received by the rods and cones, so we begin with a certain amount of deletion even before the brain begins the process of evaluation.

I am sure the brain doesn't delete anything it perceives, and at the same time I am sure it sorts input for current importance. My brain has already learned that if I see somebody who is a foot and a half taller than I am, I should probably go into my "nice mode" and quickly get into rapport with him. (Laughter) For very good reasons, the brain evaluates important survival information very quickly. Does that answer your question?

Tim: Pretty much. Just as there is a certain deletion at the rods and cone stage, there is some of that information that gets sorted out and is not passed on. Does that process of deletion continue with the analyzers, organizers, and evaluators?

A: Yes, the brain sorts for important information in a particular context.

M: To put it in Neuro-Linguistic language, it is deleting, distorting, and generalizing. It is how we make meaning out of what is coming in. We delete information to prevent being overwhelmed, we distort it through our filters, and we make generalizations about the meaning as the information goes from input to response.

Linda: If I get this correctly, the first part of the process is mechanical, visual, and then it becomes perceptual.

A: Yes, in the beginning, the process is very mechanical, it's just input. When the input gets to the portion of the brain where it is initially sorted into the separate hemispheres, the input is still the same. It is not until the information goes from the analyzing cells, to the organizing cells, and on to the cells that co-ordinate the input into perceptual meaning that it becomes an emotional evaluation.

Linda: Is it at that point where we can learn to insert personal choice by being aware of both perceptions?

M: Yes, exactly.

Linda: Beautiful. This is going to give me more choices in working with my clients.

M: That's what I have discovered. I am using it with nearly every client in my private practice. It is having a significant impact for my clients, whether they are dealing with a panic attack, a learning strategy, an identity crisis, or a relationship issue.

I had one client that came to me because his new job required him to speak in front of large groups. He knew he was well qualified for his new position, but had a sense of anxiety whenever he thought about being in front of a group. By using The Hemispheric Eye Model, he was able to identify an event that had been out of his conscious awareness that was causing his anxiety.

Once he was able to access the information that had previously been out of his conscious awareness, he could bring it into consciousness where he could learn from it. He was then able to do the emotional healing that allowed him to be comfortable while speaking in front of a large group of people.

We will share other specific examples throughout the seminar about how this new model works for emotional healing.

Understanding
Hemispheric Specialization

A: We want to be careful here that we are not confusing the use of The Hemispheric Eye Model (THE Model) with psychoanalysis, and yet it has been said that the goal of psychoanalysis is to make the unconscious conscious. The techniques used with THE Model have the ability to do that quickly and easily.

It is important to recognize the difference between a *model* and a *technique*. A model applies to, and can be used in, many different contexts. A technique is a sequence of steps designed to achieve a specific outcome.

Submodalities and *neurological levels* are also good examples of models because they can be applied to many different areas. (See glossary for definitions of submodalities and neurological levels)

One of our main purposes here is to help you become so familiar with the concepts of The Hemispheric Eye Model that you can use them in a variety of situations.

M: THE Model helps us understand what is happening, out of our awareness, that is running our internal programs. What THE Model offers is, "OK, so this is what we are conscious of in our mind's eye." Now the question becomes "What else is there? What's in the other mind's eye that might be useful?"

A: It's also about having the ability to integrate the information completely by choice. I can react in my habitual way to a fear or a challenge situation, or I can shift over to see what information is in my other hemisphere.

M: Another good question is "What are the resources the other part of my brain may have?" The intent is to pull together the experiences of both hemispheres. The Hemispheric Eye Model is a precise way of finding out what is in our unconscious perception of a situation. Then we can bring it up to consciousness, shift it, and then let it go back to automatic in a way that leaves us more resourceful and with more choices.

Chris: Would this be where the difference comes between being optimistic or pessimistic?

M: I think that filter comes from our experience. Optimism and pessimism are contextual filters that are supported by beliefs. Any time we learn a new way to think we are creating a new strategy, as well as unhooking old beliefs.

If there have been times during the formative years when it was not OK to be attending to an emotional state, or it was not safe to think and be in a thoughtful state, the filters often become habituated. For myself, one filter was the frustration I went through trying to learn algebra. We will talk this afternoon when we do the memory strategy part of our workshop, about what it was like knowing that I was smart, and yet experiencing the frustration of saying to myself, "I don't have a clue about what I just read!" Now I know that there was no translation from the printed page into my visual system.

At first, it was difficult for me to understand how to get the other mind's eye to "see" the pictures. There was a sense of being sure the image was in there somewhere, I just was not seeing it consciously. It took a willingness to practice and knowing that, if I just stayed with it long enough, eventually I would be able to have both images. Then one morning I woke up and an image of a cat appeared in my mind's eye, and suddenly there was also the word "cat" under the picture. I said, "Wow, I can see the word!" It was so exciting, and it is still there!

The other day we got a new cell phone, and Al told me the phone number. In the past I had never been able to consciously create pictures from someone just telling me something. As Al told me the number it was like a typewriter in my brain, I just saw the new phone number being printed as I looked up to my left. I still remember it precisely whenever I need the number. I am so excited about this, because now I can hold precise digital information in my mind's eye and remember it days and weeks later, when I choose to recall the information, which I had never been able to do before.

In the excitement of my new ability to remember numbers, I have changed some old limiting beliefs about myself as a person who can't learn algebra. Now I would have to say that I am optimistic about learning algebra, if I ever find a need for it in my life. (Laughter)

I encourage people who have not been able to have control of their internal pictures to practice. It does work, and it works even better when we are able to use both sides of our brains.

A: There is an example I like to use to explain how the two hemispheres of the brain bring information together to create a single experience. When Marilyn and I got married, there were certain things that I brought into the condo. I had a bedroom set, a toaster oven, and an easy chair. She had certain things already there, such as a couch and a microwave. I had a TV and she did not. We both brought valuable items to the household. If I had brought the same things she had, we would have two couches, two microwaves, and two refrigerators.

M: And no TV.

A: It is a lot like when couples get together and they bring individual qualities into the relationship. Marilyn has certain skills and resources and I have others, so we are bringing the best of each of us together to make a full unit. The brain is similar in that it is taking information coded in the left hemisphere and information coded in the right hemisphere and bringing it all together to create one perception.

M: Information can flow back and forth. Not only can I see a fluffy image, but I can also see the digital word. The important thing is that now I have more ability to use left brain filters, right brain filters, or both.

A: When some people get stuck, there is often a strategy in place that they have rehearsed and practiced that helps them stay in a stuck place. What is missing are these: They don't have the information about the strategy to help them get unstuck. They have not rehearsed the new strategy. They may not know that it is possible to change. Once there is a strategy in place to develop the flexibility, and someone has practiced it for a while, that person will have more choice. We grow up unconsciously modeling particular individuals, and sometimes we don't develop the kind of flexibility that allows us to have the information from both hemispheres.

M: So just for fun, let's experience an unconscious pattern. Everybody put your hands together, interlocking your fingers, and just notice which thumb is on top. Comfortable and easy, isn't it? Now switch hands to reverse which thumb is on top, and notice how weird that feels. Now go back to the comfortable way, and then back to the new way. If we were to continue this about ten to fifteen times, you would not be able to tell the difference. (The group continues to switch hands as Marilyn keeps talking)

My son broke one hand playing football, and he said, "Oh, mom, I can't do my schoolwork." Being a mom, I said "Guess what? You have a left hand, you will do your schoolwork with your left hand, and it will work fine." He was able to write with his left hand, but not as well. As he practiced over the time he had the cast on, he got better at writing with his left hand.

Jay: I had a similar experience. I broke my hand during my junior year in high school. I found it put me on the sideline for sports, and it forced me to write with my other hand. I found that, because it forced me to write with a different part of my brain, my grades changed in just the way that you would expect from what we have learned so far. I got better at things that I had not previously been good at, because I was now being forced to write with the other side of my body and to process with the other side of my brain.

A: Nice example. Thanks. Jay's story reminds me of something very interesting I would like to share with you. A research scientist named Marcel Kinsbourne taught volunteer test subjects to balance a small metal rod on their index finger until they were proficient at it with each hand. Next he came up with a series of test phrases for the subjects to repeat out loud while balancing the rod, using one hand at a time. Kinsbourne found that the subject's ability to balance the rod was dramatically affected while balancing the rod in their right hand as they repeated the test phrases. When they balanced the rod with the left hand, they could repeat the statement and continue balancing the rod.

Motor responses (movement) for the right side of the body are controlled by the left hemisphere, and the motor responses for the left side of the body are controlled by the right hemisphere. The major speech centers are in the left hemisphere, so the test subjects had difficulty balancing the rod with the right hand because the extra task of repeating the test phrase began to overload the conscious mind in the left hemisphere. The same side of the brain was now trying to accomplish two tasks, that in and of themselves, required multiple tracking. This caused the conscious mind to go beyond the seven (plus or minus two) items it is capable of consciously tracking at any given moment.

M: When the task was shared in the same hemisphere, the person was not able to do the task. How does it feel now? (Referring to the group still switching how they clasp their hand together)

Chris: I'm starting to lose my ability to tell which way was the natural way.

M: Interesting, isn't it? This is a good example of just how adaptable we are as human beings and that we can shift unconscious patterns.

Greg: Don't we tend to switch our dominant side at times?

A: Yes, in fact that leads us right into the next topic which, I believe, will answer your question.

Natural Shifts
in Hemispheric Dominance

A: I mentioned earlier that one of the pieces of information that led to the discovery of Internal Dominant Eye Accessing was the concept of ultradian rhythms. Ultradian rhythms are natural body rhythms that occur more than once per day. One such rhythm involves the shifting of hemispheric dominance between the right and left hemispheres of the brain. Although the time varies among individuals, this shift happens about every ninety minutes.

Milton Erickson, who was well known for his ability to recognize the fine details of a person's physiology, found that he could tell which internal hemisphere people were processing information in more dominantly by noticing their external facial features. This is an example of being able to notice external cues as they relate to internal processes. The external evidence for the shifting of ultradian rhythms for hemispheric dominance is called *face lateralization*.

(See chart C)

Example of Utradian Rhythm
For Hemispheric Dominance

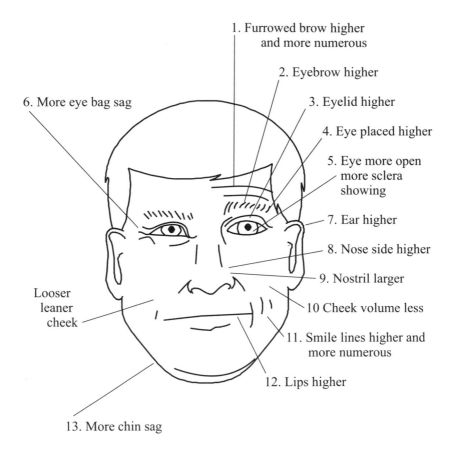

1. Furrowed brow higher and more numerous

2. Eyebrow higher

3. Eyelid higher

4. Eye placed higher

5. Eye more open more sclera showing

6. More eye bag sag

7. Ear higher

8. Nose side higher

9. Nostril larger

10 Cheek volume less

11. Smile lines higher and more numerous

12. Lips higher

Looser leaner cheek

13. More chin sag

Face lateralization: Left lifted face and mouth line suggesting right hemispheric dominance at this moment in time.

CHART C

(At this point Al and Marilyn use a volunteer participant to demonstrate an example of face lateralization. We suggest you take time to notice this phenomena as you go through your day. Chart C has been included so the reader can follow along with this example and has been drawn to represent an exaggeration of the facial features. This is an example of a left lifted face, which indicates right hemispheric dominance.)

A: So let's see, Greg, would you come up? Ok Greg, if you will stand here and just face straight ahead so that the group can see your face, and you can look back at them and notice their faces.

        As you look at Greg, notice which side of his face seems longer. Notice that there is a little more room between his left eye and the outside edge of the left side of his mouth.

Rita: You can see it really quickly.

A: Good. Also notice how the left side of his mouth is a little lower than the right side and that his left eyebrow is a little higher than his right eyebrow. Now pay attention to his ears. His left ear is a little higher than his right ear. OK, thank you Greg.

(Greg returns to his seat)

        Some of these specific features may not be as dominant in some people as in others.

M: Especially if you are in the middle of shifting from one hemisphere to the other.

A: A great place for a pattern interrupt with hypnosis is when people are shifting hemispheric dominance. Because they are shifting, their brains are a little bit confused just for a moment, so it is much easier to confuse the conscious mind. That brief confusion is something we all go through. For example, if we are in class for too long and we don't give you a break and you start getting a little drifty and have difficulty concentrating, it's likely you are going through a shift in your ultradian rhythms.

Eric: Or, a naturally occurring trance state.

A: Right. As I have been watching movies, I have been checking for ultradian rhythm shifts because I know they don't film a movie all at once. I watched a movie with John Candy through different scenes to see if I could detect his ultradian rhythm shift. I noticed that his face lateralization seemed to stay on the same side. As I recall, he had a left lifted face. I also saw that sometimes it seemed to be not as left lifted. He still maintained his left lifted face, but not as much. That indicated to me that he did shift, just not all the way over to a right lifted face.

M: So, in calibrating a particular individual, you may not see their eyebrow shifting over and becoming higher than the other one, it may just lower slightly in their rhythm. Their higher eyebrow may always be their higher eyebrow. So again, we look for the uniqueness of the individual and how they are doing the rhythm shifting.

A: Recently, I went to a chiropractor to experience cranial-sacral massage, and it really put me into a wonderful state. I remember thinking, "Life is good."

M: When he got off the chiropractor's table he said he felt kind of spacey. Al usually has a right lifted face (longer between the outside of the right eyebrow and the right side of the lip), indicating left hemispheric dominance. When I checked his face he had shifted over to a left lifted face, indicating that he had shifted to his right hemisphere.

A: Personally, I have a right lifted face more often, which makes sense because I tend to be more analytical with a logical, linear thinking pattern.

M: In fact, I have noticed that sometimes when I ask Al a question, he will squint with his left eye.

A: When I concentrate, I think I am unconsciously looking for that linear access in the brain.

There are three important things to remember regarding ultradian rhythms. First, we do shift hemispheric dominance. Second, there are external cues as to when that shift is occurring. Third, ultradian rhythms, as they relate to hemispheric dominance, have an influence on the formation of imprints.

An imprint comes from an event in the past in which we formed beliefs about ourselves and the world in general. Some beliefs are empowering, while other beliefs may be limiting. The hemisphere people are in more dominantly will affect their perception of the event, and therefore, what beliefs they form about themselves based on that event. If, at the time of the event, I am more dominant in my left hemisphere, the perception will be coded more dominantly as a logical, linear sequence of facts. If I am more dominant in my right hemisphere at the time of the event, it's going to be coded more as to how it relates to me as a person, fully associated into the event.

A personal example of how hemispheric dominance can influence perception is that getting out of the water became a matter of my survival on three different occasions. For two of the events, there didn't seem to be anything scary once the danger had passed. My perception of the other event was much different. Even though I had always enjoyed swimming and other water related activities, I was afraid to get back into the water. Fortunately, I took the time that day to reacquaint myself with the water slowly, and the debilitating part of the fear soon went away. I still love swimming and being in the water because I was able to change the belief that I couldn't be safe in the water. My new belief is that *I can* be safe in the water as long as I take the appropriate precautions.

Of course, there is no way for me to calculate which hemisphere I was in more dominantly during each of those events. My guess is that for the two that did not form a limiting belief I was more dominant in my left hemisphere, and for the more emotionally charged event I was more dominant in my right hemisphere.

Many factors need to be considered as to how we form beliefs, and hemispheric dominance is one of those factors.

Ila: Do you find a correlation between which hemisphere people are in and their ability to change unwanted behaviors?

A: Yes, and by having conscious access to specific hemispheric functions, we can begin to streamline the process of change. According to Richard Restak in his book The Brain-The Last Frontier, there is evidence that new or unfamiliar information is processed more in the right hemisphere. (See Chart A) Once that information becomes more familiar, the left hemisphere becomes more responsible for the function. If something is unfamiliar to me, like an exercise program, the information is going to be processed more in the right hemisphere because it's new. Once the new concept has become routine, and accepted as fact, the left hemisphere will start to take over the function.

In the book <u>Psycho-Cybernctics</u>, Maxwell Maltz says that it takes 21 days of repetition for a new behavior to become a habit. Based on hemispheric specialization it seems to be the left hemisphere that takes "pretending as if" and turns the new behavior into "just is."

Think about addictions for a moment. For example, people that quit smoking often have difficulty for about three weeks, which is 21 days. Pretty soon the left brain is starting to get the idea that it belongs to a person who doesn't have the behavior of smoking. The habits are changed, and the cues or triggers that used to lead to that old behavior of smoking are also changed. The information is starting in the right hemisphere as a new behavior of doing something other than smoking, then the new behavioral choice comes over to the left hemisphere as a fact.

What happens in a situation when a person has difficulty in changing the behavior of smoking I refer to as *rapid sequential incongruence*. After the right side of the brain says "I can see me not smoking in that situation," the left brain, which has access to habit memory, speaks up with "Oh yeah, but I already know you do smoke." **Until people make that new behavioral choice enough times for the left brain to believe that the new behavior is a fact, they have an internal conflict**.

Eric: Giving new information to the right brain is better done metaphorically or poetically.

A: Beautiful. That's what causes an isomorphic metaphor to work so well; the story is just a little off the actual situation, yet it is similar. Again, it is the deleting, distorting, and generalizing process. The right hemisphere looks for "what is the same?" and "how does this relate to other situations?" This is where metaphor is created, and lives long enough for the left brain to say "Oh, yeah, that makes sense." This is why future pacing is so valuable.

Gail: My experience seems to be that I am very linear and very literal. Spatial is very difficult for me, and I don't find myself using poetic language, so I'm left brained. If people are left brained, are they more likely to identify themselves by what they do?

M: First, I think it serves our purposes here better if we avoid labeling that you are a "left–brain" or a "right–brain" person. It is where you are more dominantly processing specific information and how you can get the holistic sense of using both hemispheres that we are more concerned with this weekend. I really want to avoid labels of "you're a this, or you're a that." We all have access to both sides of the brain.

To answer Gail's question, what seems to govern where we spend most of our processing time is "where do we feel safe?" We will most likely feel safe in habitual processing patterns.

An example that comes to mind is of a bicycle built for two. Often the person in the front may be doing most of the pedaling, and the person in the back is just coasting along or giving a token pedal. The person in the front is more dominant. If you have ever had this experience, you know that the bicycle goes faster and smoother when both people are doing their fair share balancing the load, so to speak.

A: Keep in mind, or should I say keep in both minds, that the corpus callosum is a network of over 50-million fibers or connections. If each fiber has the ability to fire 20 times per second, the corpus callosum is capable of transferring in the neighborhood of one billion impulses from one hemisphere to the other in an instant. So, even though we are more dominantly focused in one side of the brain, the two sides still have an incredible ability to communicate with each other.

Directing Your Brain on Purpose

A: The next piece we are going to explore is related to Eric's statement about connecting with the right hemisphere through metaphor and poetic language. In other words, how do we use our language to point the brain in a specific direction? Once again, more of your visual access is going to be in the right hemisphere for creating and processing unfamiliar information. Linear facts are going to be in the left side where sequencing and most of the language centers are.

Later, when we do our processes, we will want to know how to direct the brain to the most resourceful place for the explorer (client). For example, if I say to the group, "I want you to get a picture," or "just imagine for a moment," your brains are automatically shifting attention to the right hemisphere. If I say, "I would like to ask you a question," your attention will shift to the left hemisphere where most of the speech centers are located.

M: I will give you an example of what can happen when we inadvertently direct someone's attention to a hemisphere that we may not want them to be in. I am sure that those of you who work with couples will verify this. The couple comes in and one or the other, often times it is the wife, says: "I just want to talk. I want him to listen to me. I want him to hear me. I ask to sit down and have a half hour conversation in the evening and he flips on the TV." What the woman is trying to say is: "I want relationship. I want connection. I want to feel the warm fuzzies." Well, where is she directing his brain? Where are the major speech centers? They are in the logical linear side, aren't they? So she's asking for relationship and connection, and her words are directing her partner into linear thinking.

A: Of course, this holds true for a man or woman, there is no gender differential for this pattern.

M: I just happened to pick this example because it tends to be what I see most often in my practice. If the person could learn to speak their truth and say, "You know, I really want to feel connected with you," or "I want us to just sit and have time together, and I want to feel the warmth of you," they are more likely to get the results they want. On the other hand, if I turn to Al and say, "I want to talk about something," he immediately goes into a defensive posture.

A: It makes me wonder: "What now? What's wrong?" I worked at the phone company, I know what "I want to talk to you" means. (Laughter)

M: Language can trigger old anchors too, so it is also important to notice how we are directing someone's brain by how we phrase our words.

Eric: So you are also triggering way back in time with the imprint of somebody saying, "I want to talk to you."

M: Right. Which is exactly like this, with finger pointing, (shaking her finger) "I want to talk to you."

A: You are not only getting the imprint, which is powerful enough in and of itself, you are also pointing the person's brain to focus with a linear, more dissociated tendency. She wants to associate. She wants connection and relationship with this individual, and she is in effect saying, "Get over in your left brain while I try to get close." There is an incongruent or conflicting message.

I want you to have an experience. I'm going to make a statement, and I want you to pay attention to your internal response. Everybody keep your left eye open and cover your right eye with your hand. OK, ready? (Al makes the statement in a stern voice.) "You're not doing this right."

(Brief pause)

Notice your internal response to that statement.

(Brief pause)

Now, everybody switch and keep your right eye open and cover your left eye with your hand. Notice your internal response as I repeat the statement. (Al repeats the statement with the same volume and tonality.) "You're not doing this right."

Mike: "Oh, yeah?"

Rita: That was really different.

A: Right, now take just a moment to notice *what* was different. What was your internal experience with that?

Gail: On the last one, I felt more emotional reaction.

Rita: Me too. When my right eye was open it was much more emotional.

Don: When you said it the first time, the tone or phrase seemed different.

M: Right, the tone or phrase *can* seem to be different. Since I knew what Al was going to do, my job was to calibrate the consistency of the statement to make sure that the tone, tempo, volume, and words were as close as possible to the same. I didn't notice any difference between the two statements.

Mike: The second time was a lot more serious than the first.

Rita: I thought the first time was more serious.

Gail: For me, there was a level of dissociation when you said it the first time.

A: Some of you report that the first time was more emotional, and others feel that the second time was more emotional. The response people notice when we do this exercise varies among individuals, and most people *do* notice a difference. The more intense the statement, the more noticeable a person's internal response will be.

Mike: We all covered the right eye the first time when Al said it, why is the response different?

M: Remember that this is unique for each individual. We are noticing that individual's response. When you are driving down the freeway and someone cuts you off sometimes your response is "Have a nice day," and other times your response is "You jerk!" We are finding that which hemisphere of the brain you are in, based on your Ultradian Rhythm, can make a huge difference in your perception of an event.

A: It's interesting to notice that you didn't cover an ear, you covered an eye. Your internal experience from receiving the auditory input was different depending on which eye you covered. Remember, when we talk about the evaluation coming from the coordinating cells in the brain and on to the amygdala, there is a "see-hear" connection of our experience.

M: Which is why it is so important to understand how to use our language to get the results we intend.

A: This is another way to have flexibility in our communications, beginning with the knowledge that yes, it does make a difference. If I were to be talking to Marilyn, looking into one eye, and saying, "I really care about you," and she is not responding to the message the way I intend it, I might want to focus in her other eye and notice what response I get. Excellent communication involves noticing what works and then being flexible enough to incorporate what works best into our behaviors. **Which eye you are looking into as you speak is going to have an influence on another person's internal perception, at some level.**

Eric: So, you are also saying there is a congruency that has to come along with the words. If you are going to be saying something that's negative, you better look negative as you say it. If I hear somebody making a statement that they are angry, and there is no congruency that they are really angry about something, I am going to get a mixed message.

A: That is an excellent point; however, what we are saying in this example is to notice how different the other person's response is depending on which eye you focus on as you are speaking to them. Then be flexible enough to alter your communication to get the response you want.

What we are showing in the example of saying the same statement to each eye separately is that there is a visual and auditory link in our perceptions that is influenced externally.

As for the part of Eric's comment regarding verbal and non-verbal congruence, repeated incongruence in communication can lead to several problems such as ambivalence. An example of how incongruence can lead to ambivalence is the parent who takes away a pencil that their child is running with and angrily says, "Don't you know I love you?" The child is getting one message verbally and a different message non-verbally through volume and tonality. It's the confusion from that mixed message that can create ambivalence if the pattern continues over a period of time.

M: There is a concept we use called *psycho-geography* that in part refers to which side a person is more comfortable communicating from, the right or the left. The question becomes, from which side are they going to receive information better? For some people it will be the right side and for some the left.

One theory is, in the past, a person may have been physically abused on one side or a parent yelled at them or they might have a critical voice on one side. We are finding there may be another reason for people having a preferred side. Like for myself, I'm a telephone ear on the left side person. I can hear out of my right ear, it's just not nearly as comfortable. And look how we are standing. (Al is standing to the left of Marilyn.) I prefer to have someone on my left side, as opposed to my right side.

Larry: I didn't notice a difference with either my right or my left eye covered. Is that something that would change by increasing my sensitivity or awareness?

A: Possibly. I'm not sure it is as much about internal sensitivity as it is about the emotional sensitivity to that particular statement. For some people just saying something like, "Your shirt looks funny," will elicit a notable difference in their internal response. With other people, I need to be almost mean or rude for them to notice much of a response. You know you are safe here, so there is a presupposition that you will be treated with respect.

By feeling safe in this seminar, you are already recognizing that when we say we want you to have an experience, then say something in a critical way, it's a role-play. And even as a role-play, most of the group noticed that it made quite a difference. As for Larry, my guess is that he had already discerned that this is going to be an interesting experience and that there is nothing personal intended. If a critical statement were made out in a real world context, he might notice more of a difference.

Susan: If you know you are about to be confronted by someone who is probably going to say something you won't like, is there a value in closing your right eye if you respond highly emotionally with your right eye?

A: Technically, yes. My guess is, however, that it may not be socially acceptable to put your hand over your eye or go into an extended wink when your boss approaches. (Laughter)

What I have learned to do, because I have been practicing with my internal eye, is set my focus internally to the most comfortable side.

Having more control of which hemisphere I am accessing more dominantly has made life easier for me. I believe that with practice everyone can consciously direct his or her attention to a specific hemisphere.

How to Determine Eye Dominance

A: Now we are going to learn how to determine our external dominant eye. Before we do, it is important to understand that this is only a rehearsal for what we are going to do next with your internal dominant eye. It is kind of like using training wheels. Once you can ride a bike without them, they no longer serve a purpose. Remember that this is only an external example of what is happening internally.

There are two important reasons to experience and understand the external dominant eye. The first is to demonstrate that when we look at something, it may appear that we are seeing the object with both eyes, which is true. And it is also true that we are seeing the object more dominantly with one eye or the other. The second reason is to let the unconscious mind have a rehearsal for accessing internal images which may be out of our current conscious awareness.

The easiest way to determine your external dominant eye is to point at an object then alternate closing one eye then the other. Notice which open eye keeps your finger pointing directly at the object.

(Al draws a dot about two inches in diameter on the flip chart. For those who are reading this book, simply pick out an object about 15 to 20 feet away that is between 2 to 4 inches in diameter. Using the index finger of either hand, simply point at the spot you have chosen.)

I will demonstrate by pointing to an imaginary dot behind you in the back of the room. I am going to keep my head straight, so that both eyes are the same distance from the object, and keep my head from moving or tilting as I point at the object. As I do that, I am going to hold my finger on the object. Then I am going to close one eye and then open it, then switch to close the other eye and open it. Next I notice which eye keeps my finger on the spot. Go ahead and do that much now. (The group does the activity) Notice how your finger will jump off the dot with one eye and it will stay on the dot with the other eye.

Gail: My dominant eye changes when I point with my other hand.

A: What can happen sometimes is that we are not pointing from directly in front of our eyes. What we have found is that because our shoulders are a little further away from the center of our focus point, we have a tendency to hold our finger a little to the side of the hand that we are pointing with. So it can change. The important part of this exercise for our purposes here is that we have an awareness that we are seeing externally more dominantly with one eye.

As you look at the object it clearly seems as though you are seeing it with both eyes, and you are. You are, however, seeing it more dominantly through either the left or right eye.

Checking external eye dominance is just a rehearsal for what to expect when we visualize internally. When I look at that dot internally, maybe I am going to think at first that I am seeing it with both eyes. That is a normal perception. If I allow my unconscious mind to get a sense of which eye is more dominant internally, I will find that I have one eye that is seeing it more dominantly than the other.

M: Now, close your eyes and visualize the dot, and then notice which eye internally you are seeing the dot with.

A: Now practice allowing your focus to shift so that you are seeing the dot with your *other* internal eye.

Ron: When I point at the dot, I come up left eye dominant externally, but when I just sit here and look at the dot, my perception is that I have more awareness on the right side of me than on the left side.

A: I did an experiment in Newton, Kansas where Marilyn and I had gone to train Core Transformation®. We arrived a day before the training began, and Marilyn was doing some client work. I was still in the early discovery stage for THE Model, and I wanted to see if I could change my external dominance. I put a patch over the right side of a pair of sunglasses, and spent about three hours reading. I decided to go for a walk, and while I was out walking I noticed a crow flying by. As I watched the crow, I had a sense that I was seeing it with my right eye. Since I still had the sunglasses on with the patch over the right lens, I couldn't be seeing it with my right eye.

What I learned from this experience was that my perceptions might not always be accurate when I compare my internal world with my external world. If your awareness is on the right side, my guess would be that you are seeing it with your right internal eye the way I was when I was looking at the crow.

Ron: Is my external dominant eye indicative of what my internal dominant eye is?

A: Not necessarily. We have not found that there is any correlation between external and internal dominance. There may be, but not that we have found.

Greg: When I switch internal eyes, the dot goes away.

M: Sometimes it is because we are doing something that is new to us, and our unconscious mind is not quite sure what we are asking it to do. The same thing happened for me the first couple of times I tried to switch internal eyes. Once my unconscious mind understood what I wanted to have happen, it became easier. I encourage you to continue practicing, because often times switching internal eyes will access the exact information we need to make personal changes.

A friend and colleague of ours, who had experienced THE Model, was working with a gentleman doing a reimprinting process in which visualizing a past event, usually at a very young age, is an integral part. He elicited from the client's memory a time he experienced an event that left him with a negative feeling. When the client had accessed the event, our friend asked, "Which eye are you seeing it with?" The client said, "My right eye, but I don't see anything, I just feel bad," yet he had a sense of being in his right eye. Our friend then asked, "And what do you see with your left eye?" Gesturing with both hands circularly in front of him, the client replied, "Well, there's this cloud, I can't see anything, there's just this cloud." The guide then asked, "Well, just for the heck of it, what would happen if you just took the cloud away?" When he did, there was a picture of him being abused at three years old which he had never remembered before.

Having conscious awareness of the abuse imprint that was giving him a continuing negativity at an unconscious level, he could begin the healing process. This is an example of how we can begin accessing important information that has been out of our conscious awareness, and has been influencing our behaviors at an unconscious level.

Susan: A refinement of time line.

M: If not a refinement, certainly time line work can be more useful by having more access to a person's historical events. One of the nice things about this model is its effective enhancement of current NLP processes.

A: A colleague, and highly respected NLP trainer, did an excellent job of integrating THE Model into current NLP processes at the NLP World Health Certification Training. The trainer was demonstrating the S.C.O.R.E. Model for improving eyesight. The S.C.O.R.E. Model involves spatial anchoring. The explorer (client) steps into a "location" (spatial anchor) to gather information about what originally caused a behavior or a physical symptom.

The explorer had accessed a negative feeling from when he was two or three years old. The trainer noticed that while the explorer was standing in the spatial anchor his eyes tracked to a specific location, indicating that there was an imprint image neurologically coded in that spot. As the trainer held his hand in the spot where the imprint was coded, he asked the explorer, "What's here?"

The explorer said, "Nothing, I don't see anything." The trainer had him cover one eye with his hand, and repeated, "What's here?" The explorer responded, "Nothing." Then the trainer said, "Switch, and cover your other eye with your hand." When the explorer did, he said, "Oh, it's a picture of...," and the process was then able to continue. What the trainer did so well was guide the explorer's brain to the specific hemisphere where the desired information could be accessed.

M: Another example involves a client I had who was working with getting her sense of empowerment back. She had been in a relationship that the value of had long since passed, and she finally got the guy to move out. She came in for her session and said, "I know it's over, I really don't want to see him anymore, but I keep thinking about him, and every time I think about him I really feel bad." At that point she was still hooked into the relationship in some way.

I said, "Well, just for fun, when you think about him, what image comes up?" As I was looking at her, she looked off in this direction. (Marilyn gestures up and to her right.) I asked her, "What do you see as you look over there, when you think about him?" She saw an internal image of this man who looked like she needed to take care of him. He was hurt, he was sad, he wanted to get back together, he was so kind, and he was so wonderful, right? This perception of him made her feel bad, because she was the one breaking up the relationship. She was not seeing the fact that he lied to her, he didn't come home, and he was out dating other women, among other things.

So, I said, "Which internal eye are you seeing that image with?" I had her shift it to the other eye, and when she did she said, "Oh, that's worse, the picture just started popping, everything is shaking around." I said, "Then put it back." (Marilyn gestures to the original spot.) When she put it back her whole body relaxed, and she said: "Whew! That's better." Whatever information she got by guiding her brain to shift, it agitated and loosened up the picture, it started to really jump the picture around, and when we put it back, she said: "Oh! It's over. The negative feelings totally went away."

A: Her brain started integrating the information from each hemisphere.

M: She got the information from the other side of her brain, even though it was not conscious. This is an example of where I didn't need to know and she didn't need to know consciously. Her unconscious mind was able to get some piece of information from the other hemisphere, so much so that it just went "Phsstt!" She had been sitting there in this sort of "I don't know what to do!" state of mind, then all of a sudden "It's done!" To this day, she has never mentioned him in a session again.

As we are exploring and discovering what is possible with this model, even when we are not quite sure what is happening, we are able to really loosen up stuck states just by shifting the perception of the imprint. And we are able to loosen stuck states ecologically, since we are only accessing information that the explorer already has. This process simply makes the information available to the conscious mind.

A: One of the things that I find very interesting with this process is that, with very few exceptions, like the one above, when people do shift their internal eye it calms them rather than agitates them. Remember that this is also about having choice. If you don't like the picture you have, check out the other one and choose your favorite.

Another thing I think is important to remember is, until it is safe for people to recall an emotional event, their unconscious will keep the information from becoming conscious.

One of the major presuppositions in NLP is "If what you're doing isn't working, do anything else." A new presupposition might be, **"If there's not enough information in your mind's eye, check to see what is in your other mind's eye."**

Accessing and Controlling
Internal Images

M: The examples we have given (in the previous chapter) show how beneficial it is to be able to access the information that is currently out of conscious awareness, and how quickly change can take place once we do. What we are doing with Internal Dominant Eye Accessing takes visualization techniques to a new level.

Remember how Al explained that it was "necessity being the mother of invention" that led him to discovering this process? I understand that, because for most of my life I was "mind's eye challenged." It has only been since working with Al and my internal dominant eye, that I have been able to access and maintain a sense of control with my internal images. Once those of us who have been "mind's eye challenged" develop our natural abilities to access our internal pictures, it becomes relatively simple to identify which internal eye we are seeing with, and then to shift to see what is in our other mind's eye.

As I mentioned earlier, I now use this model in nearly every client session. I have found that there seem to be two variables in people's ability to access internal images. The most important is safety. As wonderfully adaptable as we are as human beings, our unconscious minds will not show us something that is likely to be interpreted as scary or hurtful.

This is where the second factor comes in, our personal strategies. What happens is we develop a strategy for accessing memory in a way that seems to offer maximum safety. For example, rather than accessing a picture first, we check out the situation in another representational system such as auditory (words or sounds) or kinesthetic (feelings), prior to accessing the picture consciously. After we have used this type of strategy for a long period of time, we may have difficulty being aware of pictures at a conscious level at all.

A: Several years ago, I had surgery on my left ankle to repair some ligament damage. I had to wear a cast up to just below my knee for about three months. Because I didn't use the muscles in my legs for so long they began to atrophy. By the time I got the cast off, my left leg was about the same size as my arm. The good news is, after I started using my leg muscles again they grew back to their original size quite quickly.

One of the techniques being used to enhance people's ability to visualize internally, is to have them begin to be more visually attentive to their external world. This is designed to stimulate the brain to more awareness of the visual modality, in order to store and retrieve information.

M: Once a place of safety is established, an internal image can be identified. I like to begin by giving my clients an experience of their ability to access internal images by using an image that is perceived as safe. I use an example of an apple because it seems safe for most people.

A: Unless you are working with sleeping beauty. (Laughter)

M: Right, so always check ecology. (Laughter) After clients have the awareness that they can access and control their internal pictures by using the apple example, they can begin *using* their internal visual abilities. By starting with either an auditory or kinesthetic lead, and taking enough time for the picture that is associated with the sound or feeling to develop, clients are able to access internal images.

A: There is concept called *synesthesia*. Have you ever noticed how some people will say, "I see what you're saying" or "I see how you feel?" A synesthesia is when we connect one or more modalities, visual, auditory, and kinesthetic, into a single perception of an event. When we experience an event, we have more than one representational system working. We generalize the event into our preferred representational system as a method of recalling the details of the event, and the other systems are also a part of it.

The way to consciously connect the visual information of a synesthesia is to begin with the modality that the explorer is most aware of, then add the other modalities, including visual, to the experience. Adding the component parts of a synesthesia in this way can often require a degree of patience. Sometimes it can be as simple as saying, "Which internal eye are you trying to see it with?" Then have the explorer use the opposite internal eye to access the image. Remember that any time we are dealing with people's emotions and their map of reality, flexibility and ecology are very important.

Holding interest in an image is also an important factor in being able to visualize. One of the things we discovered with Marilyn was she had difficulty holding an image in her conscious awareness once she was able to see it. I asked her to get an image of an apple, and when she did it quickly started to disappear. It was as though she had the information from the image and didn't have any reason to continue focusing on it. Next I had her get a movie picture of the still image of an apple, and the image stayed a little longer before fading out. Then I asked her to get an image of the apple, and told her I was going to have her change some things about the apple. I had her put it back on the tree, then back in the orchard, and then back to just the apple. As I had her changing the information involving the image, she was able to maintain access to it.

Everybody knows what an apple looks like right? Can everybody get an image of an apple?

M: Or a sense of it, even though you may not see it on the inside yet.

A: See the apple with your mind's eye, or just get a sense of what an apple looks like. Is everybody able to do that? Good. I would like you to have that apple in the center of your visual field. Now move it up to a corner. Now move it down to the opposite corner.

M: And even though you may not be seeing the apple clearly, just have a sense of directing it where to go.

A: Now bring it back to the center. Can you make it bigger? How big can you make it? Now shrink it down. Make it small.

M: Notice what color your apple is. Is it a green apple? Is it a red delicious? Now change your apple to another color.

A: And then bring the picture of the apple back to where it began in your visual field, and make the apple any color you want it to be. Then reorient back to here. Was everyone able to maneuver the apple around in your mind's eye?

Mike: Just a little, the apple would keep fading out.

M: I understand. If I were to say, "OK, take a bite of this apple," it would be silly, because you know it isn't a real apple. Somewhere in your brain you have a sense that this is not an apple, and yet you have an internal representation of an apple, even though before we did the visualization it wasn't in your conscious awareness.

My favorite story of the kind of frustration that some people get, which I have experienced myself, happened while I was teaching Core Transformation®. One of the participants was sitting in the front row while we were exploring internal images. She was becoming slightly agitated saying, "I don't see pictures!" After about the fourth time the group went off to do an exercise, she came back and once again said, "I *still* don't see any pictures!" She was getting more and more frustrated. No matter how gentle I was with her she just was not consciously aware of her internal visual images; although her nonverbal cues, such as looking up with her eyes, indicated the visual component was there.

I knew she had three children, so when the group took a break to go to lunch, I had three members of the assisting team stand over to the side. I talked to her for a moment to see how things were going, and she said she still couldn't get pictures. I said, "You have children, don't you?" and she answered, "Yes." I asked, "How many children do you have?" and she said, "I have three." I said, "Oh, they're here!" and called the three assistants to come over. She responded with, "Those are not my children!" I asked her, "How do you know?" She said, "Well they don't *look*...." She finally had that sense of "Whew." Even though her children were not in the room, she could recognize the assistants were not her children, so she knew she must have the visual images of her children in there somewhere.

The first step in being consciously aware of internal images is to simply relax and think, "OK, somewhere in my mind I have images." I can see which car is mine, I can get back to my home, and I recognize my family, so I know I have access to internal images.

Right now if each of you thought about someone that you really liked a lot, you could probably bring up a sense of that person. You might sense the warmth that you feel when you are with them, or maybe the sound of their voice, and some of you may even see what they look like. Just let yourself come from that place of safety and think: "OK, the pictures are in there somewhere, my brain is just not used to seeing them. For some reason it has been safer to keep the pictures out of my awareness."

A: Dreams are a more obvious example that somewhere in our brains there exists the ability to access and create internal images. It is less a matter of *if* we can access internal images and more about *how* to access them. Once we have practiced accessing pictures, it becomes easier to recognize and control them for generative purposes.

Now that I have been practicing with my pictures, I have been having fun trying new things. We were on vacation with my daughter at Catalina Island. Marilyn asked me if I wanted to get a picture of Avalon Bay as we approached the island. I looked at the bay for just a moment then told Marilyn, "No thanks, I've got it." I'm actually beginning to use my new-found visual access as a personal photo album. This is a big difference from where I was less than a year ago. I admit the pictures are not as detailed as I could get with a camera, yet I still have the basic visual memory of how the bay looked as we approached. Besides, I have been saving money on film. (Laughter)

M: I have another story about the value of accessing internal images and how it affects our perceptions. I went to Europe and worked with a man for six days on his personal issues. He had prepared several pages of issues he wanted to resolve. We began working through the problems, and as we completed a page I would set that list aside and continue on to the next one.

One day, as I was trying to get him to associate into a particular experience, which was proving to be difficult, I said, "Think of a beautiful sunset," and he said, "OK." As he thought of a beautiful sunset he just stood there without expression or any external evidence of what I would expect to notice from someone seeing their interpretation of a beautiful sunset.

I continued trying to get him *into* the experience, and said, "Now just imagine the colors of it and notice any sounds." Still, without expression he said, "OK." I asked, "So tell me, what's going on inside?" and he said, "I see 'BEAUTIFUL SUNSET.'" He saw the two words in his internal image rather than the picture of an actual sunset. (Good natured laughter)

My client had a really nice painting on his wall that had a little gold plaque underneath describing the scene. I said, "So tell me, you have this painting here, it's one of your favorites, you really like it, right?" He said it was one of his favorites, and began to tell me about it. I said, "Now which are you more attracted to, the little plaque that describes the painting, or the painting?" He said, "Well the painting, of course." So I said: "Which do you think your mind is going to have more fun with, actually seeing the sunset, or seeing a little plaque that says 'Beautiful Sunset'? So keep the words, that's good, and let the words become the representation of the experience."

No one had ever told him he could do that before. It wasn't that he couldn't visualize, his mind just didn't know how to do it consciously. He was being very literal, and when I said "beautiful sunset" here came the words. Sometimes that is what happens if we never learn that we can have the words and the pictures too.

At the time I didn't know it, but what I was doing was aligning his two hemispheres. He learned he could have his left brain representation of the digital words, and his right brain representation of the picture, to experience the sunset more fully. Once he recognized his options, it became easier for him to become more associated into life.

A: Please keep in mind, we are not doing anything that is new in the universe, it is already here. Our intent is to bring information from the unconscious mind into our conscious awareness in order to have more choices.

Gail: Why is it that it seems hard to remember pictures of emotional things, but it's easy to get a picture of my cat?

M: Most of our internal *parts* (aspects of ourselves) are concerned with protection, survival, and safety. If we consider for a moment, our brains are likely to protect us from situations that seem as though they may not be safe.

A friend of mine was talking about a man who was injured in a serious car accident, yet has no memory of it. His brain is using one of its many skills by having amnesia of the event. His brain may not be allowing him to have the memory of the accident if it considers it to be potentially dangerous. His unconscious mind will keep the memory out of his conscious awareness until, sometime in the future when it knows it will be safe to have the memory return. He did have the experience of the accident, and the memory of that experience is in there somewhere.

The question of accessing the memory becomes three-fold. First, is it important to know, second, is it safe to know, and third, does the person have an effective strategy to access the memory?

There is also the possibility that when a physical trauma occurs, it may cause physical damage to the brain itself in the areas that store memories. In cases involving damage to the brain, memories may not be available. What we are discussing here concerns emotional blocks that are keeping traumatic events out of conscious awareness.

Linda: What we have found with people who are suddenly hurt in the middle of a traumatic situation is that the unconscious mind puts the memory recall process on pause, and says, "We need to heal first." Once the person has healed, the brain says, "OK, I'll go back and recreate enough of the information."

A: Right. Amnesia can be a wonderful resource as long as it doesn't keep people from getting what they want. Remember as we do these processes with the internal eye, all the information is already in your brain. It's *your* brain, and all the information contained within it belongs to you. Since you are here today, you *have* survived everything that has happened in the past. We are not bringing anything in, and we are not hallucinating anything. What we *are* doing is creating an opportunity to access information that may have previously been unconscious, and making it available to the conscious mind.

(Group breaks for lunch and returns)

The Power of Perspective

A: Welcome back. As a way of reorienting back into the room after lunch, we often tell a story that relates to where we are headed.

When I took my Practitioner Training we learned about metaphors and how important they are to our experience. I started thinking about some nursery rhymes that I learned during my formative years of childhood. We have some real interesting ones like "Rock-a-Bye Baby." For anyone that may not be familiar with it, it says:

Rock-a-bye baby on the tree top
When the wind blows, the cradle will rock
When the bough breaks, the cradle will fall
And down will come baby, cradle and all

One side of my brain is creating this picture of a baby in a cradle, the wind blows, the cradle falls taking this innocent little baby with it. We even sing this to a child as we put them to sleep! I became curious what would happen if I reframed nursery rhymes. As an example, the way I reframed Rock-a-Bye Baby is:

Rock-a-bye baby on the tree top
When the wind blows, the cradle will rock.
When the wind blows hard, the cradle's set free
For this rocking baby is the seed of the tree.

Chris: Wow, that's nicer than saying a child falls to its death!

Linda: Every culture on the planet has at least one hostile lullaby, every culture.

M: When I was a child, my good night prayer was if "I should die before I wake...."

Susan: I'm not going to sleep!

A: Where does insomnia come from?   Survival! (Laughter)   I would like to share with you the first nursery rhyme I reframed, as an example of perceptual filters and how we can have one situation and more than one perception.   Once our mind has a new and more effective way to look at something, it will continue to have that new perception, at least at the level of recognizing the new perception as an option.

Another nursery rhyme I reframed is "Humpty Dumpty." The way I remember "Humpty Dumpty" from my childhood is:

Humpty Dumpty sat on a wall.
Humpty Dumpty had a great fall.
All the King's horses and all the King's men
Couldn't put Humpty together again.

A: Notice your internal response when you hear that story.

Ila: I feel sadness, frustration, and even a sense of failure.

A: I understand.   Another way to remember "Humpty Dumpty" is:

Humpty Dumpty sat on a wall.
Humpty Dumpty had a great fall.
The King's men gathered from miles around
To witness the mess now on the ground.
The King's engineers said, "We can try, or we can
Forget the rescue and get a frying pan."

Gravity took charge from where Humpty had ambled,
Now, much more than his thoughts have been scrambled.
He approached the wall to sip from solitude's cup
To meditate and become sunny side up.
He had no way of knowing before he fell
His essence would become breakfast and scattered eggshell.

When the king heard the news, his heart started achin'.
Something was missing, "Ah, yes, the bacon!"
So atop the wall he set the swine
Sausage and Ham would also taste fine.
But tomorrow he must tear down that wall
Or risk elevated cholesterol.

The King's clogged arteries would most likely kill
Or at least his physicians say that they will.
A lesson may be learned that with all the king's wealth
With poor eating habits he could not buy health.
Inability in choosing what he should eat
Would eventually lead to the king's defeat.

The kingdom has changed since Humpty's great fall
Where Humpty once fell is a shopping mall.
He knew no parents, yet had many cousins
For as we all know, eggs come in dozens.
Though his epitaph reads: "Cooked egg white and yolk,"
We find that it's Humpty who played the last joke.

Ila: That *is* different. Now I'm laughing.

A: The difference in Ila's response shows how a new perspective can shift old perceptions.

M: Did anyone have any thoughts over lunch that you might have questions about?

Chris: I noticed at lunch that it does seem to make a difference which eye I was looking at when I talked to people. Can you go over again which eye I should look at when I talk to someone?

M: What we are talking about is focusing, and how to direct another person's experience when you talk to them. A lot of the focus in NLP is how we use our language in a way that will be a positive influence. What we are doing here is similar, in the sense that now we are beginning to notice how we can use our visual focus to influence rapport in a positive way. Choosing which eye you are seeing from, and which eye you are directing the conversation into, will have an effect on the interaction.

I have noticed when Al talks to me, if it is an intense conversation, he is very directly looking into one of my eyes, and he just stays in that one eye. I am more comfortable shifting my focus back and forth between eyes. When you speak to somebody, calibrate their response to you. If you are not getting the response you want, try shifting your focus more to their other eye, and notice what response you get that way.

This level of communication is about flexibility and choice. When you are able to calibrate a client, or someone you are having an interaction with, you can focus more directly into the eye that you are getting the desired response from.

Eric: Would you talk to the right eye for emotional states and metaphor?

M: It would depend on the person you are talking to, noticing their nonverbal responses. It depends on that individual's perceptual filters.

Λ: There is a prerequisite for flexibility anytime we want to establish rapport. I find that, as I am talking to someone, I can have an effect on rapport by switching my focus from one eye to the other, even though which eye I look at varies between individuals.

M: For instance, as a trainer, if I am up here and I am intently focusing on just one person in the group, the rest of the group might start to feel excluded. If I am alternating my eye contact to include different people, I am able to encompass the entire group. Similarly, if you are talking to a person and you are looking from one eye to the other, it is going to bring in both hemispheres more than if you just focus into one eye.

Ron: When I calibrate a person I'm working with in my hypnotherapy practice, I look for which of their representational systems (visual, auditory, or kinesthetic) is most out of their conscious awareness. When I want to suggest that they go into a trance state, I go through that avenue. This concept is something I can stack on top of that for effectiveness.

Tim: I know you said we can direct a person to a specific hemisphere with our language. Have you been able to use language to shift hemispheres for people who have auditory as their preferred system?

M: Actually, yes. An interesting thing happened during a client session that was a little different than what we talked about earlier today. We discussed how to point the brain to a specific hemisphere by saying, "I want to talk to you about something," or "I want you to get a picture." These are examples of directing the brain's attention to a specific hemisphere. This story is an example of how our words can sometimes keep us stuck.

My client, who has joint custody of her children, was having difficulty setting and maintaining her personal boundaries with her ex-husband. According to my client, he was being verbally abusive every time they had an interaction involving their children. She was having a hard time setting boundaries because she had a little voice that said, in kind of a sheepish way, "I'm just so *grateful* to him." Yet that was exactly the attitude that was keeping her from setting appropriate boundaries. I asked her, "What would be another word for grateful?" She chose the word *recognize*, and changed her statement to, "I *recognize* that he helped do things for me in my life."

The word *recognize* immediately put her in a different state, her posture changed to being more upright, and she shifted into a more linear, non-emotional response. Now it's more matter of fact. "Oh, I *recognize* that this was a value in my life." She went from being stuck to being resourceful, just by shifting that one word.

A: In this example, "grateful" was represented in the right hemisphere, and "recognize" was represented in the left hemisphere. Words in and of themselves have a limited ability to represent the perceptions of an experience. If we are limited to the cognitive perceptions from only one hemisphere of the brain at a conscious level, we are limited to the choices we have in responding to an event or a situation.

When People Push Your Buttons

A: I would like to move on to an exercise now, so you can have an experience of what is possible with your other mind's eye. We mentioned earlier how what we see, hear, and feel creates our overall experience, or emotional evaluation, of a particular event.

Our experiences are driven by the qualities of the modalities, known as submodalities. For example, some submodalities of the visual modality are: color or black and white, where we see the image in space, and whether the picture is a movie or a still.   Often times, submodalities can have as much, or sometimes more of, an effect on our experience than the content of the image.

M: As with other NLP techniques, the more we pay attention to the specific submodalities, the more accurate our perceptions will be. For our purposes here, there are certain submodalities that seem to be important to notice while exploring the internal dominant eye.   There may very well be others that play an important role in a person's experience. The list we offer here are the ones that we have found to consistently have an integral effect with THE Model.

A: The visual submodalities that seem to play an important role are location, size, brightness, framed or panoramic, color or black and white, clarity, focus, and movie or still. One of the most important distinctions is referred to as being *associated, disassociated,* or *dissociated.*

Associated is being in the experience, seeing through your own eyes, hearing in your own ears, and feeling your own feelings. Disassociated is associated, but from somewhere else into a different perspective. Dissociated is numb, cutoff, or out of the experience. Although associated or disassociated are more commonly linked to the visual modality, we find there can be a sense of associated or disassociated in the auditory and kinesthetic channels as well. Just be aware that it is possible to have these distinctions in more than one representational system.

M: For auditory, the words themselves will often change when the explorer switches internal eyes. In the auditory channel you will want to check both internal and external auditory. For internal auditory, check for self-talk and any other sounds the explorer may be hearing. Sometimes people hear an internal "Yuck." For external auditory, check background sounds and what another person might be saying. Some auditory submodalities to notice are location, tone, tempo, volume, rhythm, monaural or stereo, clarity, and, of course, the content of the words.

A: In the kinesthetic modality there are three types of feeling. The first is *tactile,* which is the sense of touch and temperature. The second is *proprioceptive,* which has to do with movement and visceral feelings. The third is an overall evaluation of the input from all sensory channels as they pertain to each individual's unique filtering system, known in NLP terms as the *meta-k* or *meta-kinesthetic.* Meta means about or beyond. In more common terms, meta-k simply represents the emotional evaluation of an experience.

Some submodalities to elicit for tactile and proprioceptive feelings are location, pressure, texture, temperature, and balance. If the beginning picture gets a kinesthetic response in a particular area of the body and then changes when you shift internal eyes, it is a good indication that there has been a significant internal shift. These are some of the submodalities we will pay particular attention to. Obviously the more information you have, the more precise you can be with your work. If somebody offers you more information, go ahead and use it. (See appendix for a more complete list of submodalities.)

As we mentioned earlier, the modalities of olfactory (smell) and gustatory (taste) have been grouped in with the kinesthetic modality. If appropriate, elicit the submodalities for smell and taste.

M: What we often do with submodalities is what we call "map across." If we have a situation that is not working very well, we transfer a submodality distinction from the image of a situation that is working well, into the image of the challenging situation. If we have a picture of a situation where we really want to add some energy, and the picture is in black and white, it might make a difference if we just change it to color.

A: What we are looking for is, what is in our current awareness, and what information is in the image in our other mind's eye that may be out of our conscious awareness. When I get two pictures, they are going to be different, and I am going to have a different evaluation from them. Noticing what submodalities are in our images from a positive resourceful situation, that are not present in a challenge situation, will help identify what our individual driver submodalities are.

A *driver submodality* is a distinction that, when changed, instantly makes a noticeable difference in our response to a given situation. To me, brightness is very important.

M: Brightness doesn't have much effect for me, whereas location is crucial.

A: Sometimes the best way to understand something is to see an example of it, so I would like to demonstrate "The Hemispheric Eye Foreground-Background Process."

The purpose of this process is to have a more resourceful initial internal response to a person who "pushes your buttons".

Does anybody have a person that, when you see them or think about them, you kind of feel, "yuck," and you would like to have more choice as to how you respond to them? (Al gestures to one of the participants raising her hand) OK, Linda, would you be willing to play?

Linda: Always.

A: Great, come on up.

(Linda comes up to the platform and stands next to Al. Al takes a moment to establish rapport with Linda and to make sure she is comfortable in front of the group.)

A: Normally, the first thing I would do is explain the external dominant eye so she has that understanding, and then explain that there is also an internal dominant eye. Since Linda already has that experience, we are going to bypass that step for this demonstration.

OK Linda, I don't need to know who the person is, just go ahead and get an image of the person. (Linda nods yes.) So, as you look at this image, where do you see it in space? Where is the picture located?

Linda: Straight ahead, about 20 feet away.

A: So, it's out about 20 feet. Is it in color or black and white?

Linda: Color.

A: Notice the quality of the color and what the different colors are. (Linda nods) Is the picture framed, or is there a border around it?

Linda: No, it's not framed.

A: No frame, alright. Is it panoramic?

Linda: No, just out there.

A: Are you in that picture?

Linda: No.

A: Notice all of the other visual submodalities, like size and brightness, and just be aware of those.

Linda: Life size. Just the head, however.

A: Just the head. All right. Notice how high it is. Is it about eye level? (Al estimates that the image is eye level from observing where Linda is looking)

Linda: MmmHmm.

A: Are there sounds externally from the image?

Linda: MmmHmm.

A: You don't need to share the words unless you want to. Just be aware of the overall essence of the sound, the volume, and, if there are words, what the words are saying. Maybe even notice the quality of the voice or the sounds.

Linda: I can hear it!

A: You got it! Right. Now check for any internal sounds, maybe self-talk. If there is internal dialogue, notice the quality and volume and what the words are. You can share them or keep them private, it's your choice.

Linda: Well, I'll share. My internal voice says, "You sh_t!"

A: "You sh_t!" Yeah. OK. So I want you to get a kinesthetic sense of the feelings. Is there a feeling somewhere in your body that goes with this image? (Linda nods yes.) Can you describe that feeling for me?

Linda: A sense of loss and woe, a sense of rage, a sense of being mistreated and abused. A sense of nostalgia, loss.

A: Nostalgia, and loss. OK. Where do you feel that in your body? (Linda gestures with both hands to the solar plexus area, mid-range between her stomach and chest.) Right at the solar plexus. Okay, so now I would like you to get a sense, or maybe you are already aware, which internal eye are you seeing that image with?

Linda: Right.

A: Good. So, checking inside, and in a way that is just right for you, I would like you to allow your unconscious mind to shift, so that when you think of the person this time you are thinking of them, and seeing them, with your left internal eye.

Linda: It's bouncing back and forth.

A: It's bouncing back and forth? Alright, just stay with that for a moment as you allow your unconscious mind to continue accessing the image in your left internal eye.

Linda: (Brief pause) Left.

A: OK. Do you have the image in your left eye now? (Linda nods yes) What's that picture like?

Linda: Sepia tone. Smaller. Full body and very small.

A: Full body and very small, and it's sepia tone (brown). What about the location of this picture? Where do you see it?

Linda: It's smaller and it's in the same place. It's shrinking.

A: It's shrinking. Alright. Are there any sounds associated with this second image that are coming in externally?

Linda: Yeah, I still hear the sound.

A: How do the sounds compare to how they were before?

Linda: Different. Quieter. Less sharp. And the two words coming from the image just reversed. Interesting.

A: So the words have reversed. I don't necessarily need to know what those words are, but the words coming in externally are reversed. How about the sound internally?

Linda: "Poor thing."

A: Poor thing. Interesting. Are you associated in this picture, or dissociated?

Linda: Very associated to the feelings now, but the picture is distant.

A.   Where in your body do you sense the feelings from this image?

Linda: (Brief pause) It's not there.

A: OK. So if you were to come up with an emotional evaluation for this picture, what would that be?

Linda: Neutral.

A: Neutral. Wow! So the wonderful thing about that is you have an interesting choice. You have the second picture with your left internal eye that is neutral and small, is more associated into the feelings and a voice that says, "poor thing." You also have the first picture with the right eye that is just the head of the person, with a sense of loss and rage. There is a feeling around your solar plexus, and a voice that says, "You sh_t!"

So now you have a choice of how you want your initial internal response to be when you think about, or interact with, that person. Of those two images, which do you prefer to have for your initial internal response, knowing that we will be able to keep all the information from both images?

Linda: I can't get the picture at all now.

A: When you don't get the picture, what does that feel like?

Linda: It took my picture away. (Linda laughs)

A: Which picture went away?

Linda: Both of them. That's interesting. I've got the background and the person is gone.

A: It is important to just turn inward and check ecology, because both of these pictures have information for you. The pictures are there for a reason. So check inside. For any reason, does any part of you have a concern about letting go of those two images and going with the feelings and the sense of being neutral?

Linda: Picture's gone. That's OK. (Linda nods yes.)

A: You still remember who the picture was of. Is this a person that you are going to have interactions with in the future?

Linda: Probably not.

A: Probably not. If you were to, just by some fluke, how would that be?

Linda: Very, very different.

A: Does it feel like you will be able to be in a resourceful place?

Linda: Yes.

A: Alright, thank you Linda. Would you be willing to answer any questions the group may have about your experience?

Linda: Yes, sure.

A: Are there any questions for Linda about her experience?

Tim: Were you aware of changing internal or external eyes at all while you did this process?

Linda: Yeah.   When he said shift it was really different. Very dramatic.

Tim: How did you shift?

Linda: Well, it's very clear to me that I saw the first picture with my right eye.

Tim: How did you know?

Linda: I feel it and see it. It's very definite, it was coming from here. Right from here (Gesturing to her right eye). When he said shift, that was hard. The pictures kept flipping back and forth. It was not as easy as I expected it to be. Then, when I *was* able to shift, and hold the shift, it was definitely through my left eye. The image (brief pause) I'm doing it right now. (pause) The image went from full face to full body, very small; smaller than the full face. And that was from here (Linda gestures to her left eye).

Susan: How did you do it?

Linda: It was almost like tasking my unconscious, and it just happened. I just said to myself, "I'm going to look through this one."

Susan: So you were almost not looking with an internal eye so much as an external eye.

Linda: No, it was a definitely with my internal eye. I'm imagining that person there.

A: If it was her external eye she would actually see the person, and, since the person she thought about isn't here, it is an internal image. It really *was* an internal eye that she was accessing the image with.

Linda: Right, it's definitely an internal image. They both are, and they are different.

A: What we have done is access her internal representation of the person in the first picture with the emotions connected to it, and we have said, "OK, see it with the other internal eye." When she did, she got the different emotions that were connected to the second image.

M: It doesn't matter which internal eye initially comes up with the picture. When you shift internal eyes it either goes to a calmer place, a more neutral place, or even a more agitated place. As guide in this process, my main concern is to direct people to discovering what other information they already have in their unconscious mind in order to give them a full range of choices.

The important information here is that there is a difference in our internal perception, depending on with which eye we are seeing the image. The evidence is here in Linda and her change with her new internal response. Any other questions for Linda about her experience?

A: Yes, Mike?

Mike: As I observed you going through that change, the only thing that I had in my experience, that looked like what you were going through, was a major collapsing of anchors. Was your experience similar to a collapsing of anchors?

Linda: Yes, now that you mention it, it's similar; and yet it seems much deeper

A: In collapsing anchors we take the "resource" anchor and the "challenge" anchor and collapse them into a third newly anchored response to the same stimuli. When we collapse anchors we lose or delete some of the information from the original resource and challenge situations.

With The Hemispheric Eye Foreground-Background Process, we discover (elicit) and preserve all of the information in both images, while having a resourceful internal response to the situation or trigger. I find this is crucial in setting healthy and ecological boundaries. We can now come from a place of being proactive with choices, instead of having our "buttons pushed". Good noticing, Mike.

Linda: Thank you Al. That was very, very different Good stuff.

A: Thank you, Linda. (Linda returns to her seat)

Gail: Will Linda's new perception last?

A: Yes. We find the results do last. The first time I did this process was with a friend of mine who had an issue with her supervisor. I checked with her several months after we did the process. She reported that, even though her supervisor still isn't her favorite person, my friend has been in control of her internal response during their interactions.

M: Before doing the process she was in a bad situation. By having a negative initial internal response, her problems with the boss could only escalate. Once she began coming from a resourceful state, she was able to set her personal and professional boundaries.

The Hemispheric Eye
Foreground-Background Process

A: One of the NLP presuppositions is, **people make the best choice available to them, and often there are better choices**. By finding out what is in your other mind's eye, you are adding to your choices. If those choices are better than what you have had to work with in the past, you will choose them in the future.

We are going to talk about the flexibility of the process. As we hand out the steps for The Hemispheric Eye Foreground-Background Process, which we demonstrated with Linda, you may notice at the end of the process that the steps are a little different than what we did with Linda in the demonstration. (Previous Chapter)

What usually happens in this process is that people will hold an image of the first and second picture simultaneously and be co-conscious of them. When I asked Linda, "Which picture do you prefer?" I expected her to choose the one that was more neutral. If her unconscious mind had not let both pictures simply go way, leaving the neutral feeling, we would have continued with the steps as they are outlined in the handout. If both pictures had stayed, we would make one of them foreground, and the other background, depending on which image gives her the initial internal response she would rather have.

Foreground, in this situation, is shifting the brain's attention toward the image they are most aware of consciously. Whichever picture leads a person to being more resourceful internally, just allow that picture to come up first, or to be more foreground.

Of course, I would have to check it out with Linda, but I am guessing that internally it was appropriate for both images to go away since she considers it unlikely that she will have future contact with this person. (Linda nods yes.) If this had been a person with whom she expected to have further interactions, I would have encouraged her to keep both of the images consciously, because each side of the brain has information about that person or event. We want to keep the picture with the negative response connected to it in the background as an ecological resource.

If I have someone in my life, and I have just done this process with an issue involving them, I want to be internally resourceful. I want to leave the picture that will put me in my most resourceful state in the foreground. There is a good reason the other picture gives me a feeling that goes, "Yuck. Be careful, be on guard." I will make the more resourceful picture foreground, and I will make the "Yuck" picture background.

When I have both images set up with the more internally resourceful image foreground, and the less resourceful image background, my initial internal response will be from the resourceful one. I keep all the information that is in the background image that reminds me what they did in the past that was hurtful or dangerous. If they lied, and I found out about it, that information will still be there so that I won't set myself up to be a victim by falling into old patterns.

We learn from experience in life. By using The Hemispheric Eye Foreground-Background Process in this way, we can keep what we have learned from the past and act in a resourceful way in the present. **We are not destroying any information. We are not eliminating any knowledge or experience. We are simply putting the knowledge and experience into our awareness in a way that leaves us as our most resourceful self.**

In the demonstration with Linda, she ended up with no picture of the person. If the explorer has a different strategy for resolving internal conflict than what we expect them to have based on the script, then check for ecology, and let the explorer have her reality since she is the expert on herself.

Another point in the example with Linda is that she is very experienced in NLP. My guess is that she already has effective internal strategies for dealing with her personal ecology. By asking her to go inside to check if any part of her had a concern about letting the pictures go, I was guiding her to check her own ecology. My calibration was that she was fully congruent when she said that it was OK.

M: If we don't have a choice in our internal response to a situation, or with another person, we are not in control. It can be an indication that we have lost our flexibility.

Having choice is to be able to come from a neutral or resourceful state, and to be able to set boundaries for the safety we need in a situation, or with a person, that may be a potential threat. It is a nice option to be able to come from a place of being centered, and having the conviction to say, "Yes, this is my choice."

Now for Linda, her unconscious mind chose to just leave the sense of being neutral in her body. She didn't need to have the pictures consciously available in her mind's eyes.

Remember to be flexible with your partners. If both pictures remain, which they normally do, have one become foreground, and the other one background. If it neutralizes, go with it. You don't have to follow the steps exactly as they are in the script as long as you are honoring the explorer's ecology. When you stay flexible and ecological, the script becomes more of a suggested guideline.

Gail: When you mentioned ecology and keeping the knowledge, it reminded me about something. In the past, I have allowed a particular person to do the same thing over and over again, and I have ended up going through the same kind of emotional trauma over and over again. I end up coming to a conclusion about how to react to the same person as if I had totally forgotten or deleted all that old information. I have done that over and over with my ex-husband. He could still come and do the same thing to me again.

M: That's what typically happens if we try to delete things, and don't keep the information from the past, and what we have learned from it.

A: And now Gail, you have a choice of trusting yourself to keep the information about his patterns and strategies.

The only part of an interaction we really have control over is how we respond internally to whatever is going on externally.

Gail: Yeah, I've been doing it the opposite way.

A: So, here is a way to keep that information about your ex-husband's behaviors, and be more resourceful internally.

M: I would like you to take a moment to read over the steps and make sure you understand the process.

The Hemispheric Eye Foreground-Background Process

Purpose: For the explorer to soften an initial internal response or reaction to a challenging person or situation, while maintaining the ecology necessary for safety.

1: Establish rapport and ecology for working together.

2: Have the explorer think of a challenging person with whom the explorer would like to have a more resourceful initial internal response or reaction. *Example: Supervisor, co-worker, relative, neighbor.*

3: Elicit the explorer's submodalities paying particular attention to:
Visual - Associated or dissociated, clarity, color, movie or still picture, panoramic or framed, size and location.
Auditory - Internal and external voices, volume, location, and content of the words.
Kinesthetic - Tactile, proprioceptive, and emotional evaluation.

Guide calibrates external cues, checking carefully for ecology.

4: Guide says, **"Get a sense of which internal eye you are seeing that image with."** Note response. After response, guide says, **"After checking inside, and in a way that is just right for you, shift your attention to your other internal eye, so that you will be seeing that person now with the information coded in your other hemisphere."** *Guide notes any change in external cues.*

5: Elicit any differences in submodalities, paying close attention to any shift in emotional response.

6: Identify which picture gives the explorer the most choice of responding resourcefully. Have the explorer make this image foreground and leave the less resourceful image background. *Leaving one of the pictures background preserves information and is therefore more ecological.*

7: Assist the explorer in establishing foreground-background by asking them, **"What would make the resourceful picture stand out?"** Test for response and adjust as appropriate.

8:_ Check to see what follow-up work may be needed. *Doing this process often allows issues to surface, such as limiting beliefs or negatively charged memories. These can then be dealt with using other techniques now, or at a later time.*

9:      Guide tests the explorer's new response by asking, **"When is the next time you will think about, or be with this person, and you want to have your new response?"** Have the explorer imagine being with the person, and calibrate their nonverbal response.

10:     Future pace the new choice the explorer now has to adjust internal dominant eye accessing with this person and with others in the future.

A: I find that there is more access to physiology, and therefore more neurology is involved, when you stand up as you do the process. If you sit down to do a process, you tend to dissociate more easily.

M: We have already had the experience of identifying the external dominant eye as a group. If you are going to do this with somebody else, you will want to give them a chance to determine their external dominant eye. This will give them a rehearsal for their internal dominant eye.

A: Even though it is a nice rehearsal for accessing the internal dominant eye, we have had a lot of success doing this process without a set-up or explanation. In fact, we have even done this process conversationally with instant results.

        We used this process with a friend of ours who was having a marital issue, and when we asked her, "Do you get a picture of that," she said, "Yeah." We asked, "Where do you see that picture?" She gestured and said, "It's right here." We had her shift eyes to see it with her other internal eye, and she said, "Oh, it's over here now (gesturing to a different location), that's better." She then went on with the conversation. It was a quick and easy shift. Sometimes you don't need to go through the whole process step-by-step.

Chris: So was the relationship over, or was the issue over?

M: The issue. She now had more conscious access to her internal resources to deal with the issue, instead of just being instantly angry.

A: Remember, at the end of any process we want to test to see if the explorer is in a resourceful state that is as good as, or better than, when they started. Then, as I did with Linda, check to see how it will be the next time the explorer thinks about or interacts with that person.

This process was originally designed to give a people more choice about their initial internal response to a person. This process using The Hemispheric Eye Model also works well with specific negative events, and for situations such as public speaking.

Group breaks for exercise and returns

New Perspectives

M: What did you discover?

Don: I used a memory of an event that was negative, and the pictures were similar. There was a slight change in distance, and a little more detail in the picture with my left eye. In the right eye, it was a little closer, a little bit fuzzier, and a bit more to the right. Neither one seemed to give me any major shift from the visual. What did happen though, is when I shifted eyes the sounds changed from my right ear to my left ear, and that made a big difference.

M: So, with the shifting of the sound, you got the difference. When you got that sound shift, did it shift any of the emotional evaluation of the event?

Don: Yeah. It shifted my feelings about that particular event. When we future paced it, my opinion of the person didn't change. I have no problem thinking about that event, and I still don't like the person.

M: So you loosened up that stuck place?

Don: Yes, that particular piece is fine now.

M: This may indicate that there is more involved with this person than just that one event. For now, it may be ecological to keep the overall response you are having regarding that person and to explore other techniques that will help establish boundaries, or other resources, for future interactions with that person.

It is interesting to notice how your perception of that particular situation shifted more from the sounds.

Larry: What if the person just gets a blank screen with no picture?

A: Since our brains have the ability to store and recall pictures, it is just a matter of being patient and having a strategy to recall them. We worked with a participant in Argentina during a seminar. In her particular situation, she had a picture of a blank screen, but she had a sense that there was something there. I had her build the image from her feelings and her auditory channel to get the visual representation.

M: One person just got a picture of a card that was like a playing card, except that it was blank. She wasn't able to move the card away because she didn't want to see the picture yet. There was a part of her that said, "No, I'm not ready to see it yet." In some situations, you need to build in resources before accessing information from a traumatic event. We were careful to avoid forcing anything, and by respecting the person's safety we were able to get enough information to begin adding resources. Then the person could emotionally heal from the traumatic event.

A: It gave us the information about where emotional healing work needed to be done. What I recommend you do in situations like that is chunk down to a more specific part of the issue. By accessing a more specific portion of an image, you are also teaching the brain how to have more access to internal images. As with any other skill, the more you practice the easier accessing pictures will become.

Interestingly, there have been many times when people didn't get the picture of an event until they shifted their efforts in retrieving the picture to the other internal eye.

M: Who else had an interesting experience?

Gail: When I first got the image of the person, he was huge, which he is, and right in front of me, a living, breathing..., I mean right here (gesturing about 12 inches in front of her).

M: Like, *in your face*, right?

Gail: Yeah, and breathing at me, and stinking. It was like I could actually smell him. When I was able to change eyes, he immediately shrank to very small, and his words sounded like they were coming from a mouse. I was surprised that it changed so much, because all I did was switch eyes. What is really interesting is, I am a person who usually doesn't see pictures.

M: Or, at least, you didn't see pictures in the past, right?

Gail: Yeah, it does seem like it was in the past. And it's useful to learn this process now, because we are still in litigation for some legal issues.

M: So, instead of having an initial negative response, you can deal with that situation in a more resourceful way.

A: If, when I think of a traumatic event the image is right in front of me, full blown and real as though I am reliving it, I am not going to feel safe, even though it is a past event. More likely than not, I am going to shy away from that memory. When I shy away from a memory, I go into a kind of denial of the event, and avoid doing the deep structure work that will clear the way to living in the present moment as my healthy, resourceful self.

The residual effects of a trauma will have an influence on our safety and happiness, even though what created the initial trauma may be out of our conscious awareness. Often, by simply changing which internal eye we are using, the picture moves further away, shrinks in size, and changes whatever other submodalities are helping to maintain the traumatic response. This is particularly useful whenever there is severe trauma or abuse.

When I can look at a situation a little more dissociated, from a different perspective, I can work on it from a place of relative safety. When I need information from the traumatic event, it is still available. I can put the image back the way it was when I am through with the healing, if I choose to. As long as I heal the situation, and have access to the important things I have learned from the experience, I think it would be unhealthy to have it be the way it was. Using The Hemispheric Eye Foreground-Background Process will either defuse the traumatic event quickly, or create a place of safety to work with the issue. Many times, having access to both internal images will identify an imprinted event that was previously unavailable to the conscious mind.

Susan: You are onto something really big here. Mine was a spontaneous swish, which I have never been able to do.

M: Yes, and that is what we are hearing from people, "I have never been able to do this before."

Susan: Do you think this will replace the NLP Swish pattern?

A: I don't necessarily look at this process as replacing anything. I like to think of it as adding to our toolboxes. The Swish pattern is an excellent process that has helped a lot of people.

The filter I have chosen to use for your question is "How will THE Model enhance and enrich our current skills?" We are discovering the impact of this process, and we are confident that it will act as a significant tool for eliciting ecological change in a wide variety of contexts.

M: Internal Dominant Eye Accessing has become one of those basic tools to use with whatever you are doing, to have a higher and more complete success rate. We are now able to tap into the information in both hemispheres of the brain.

The Swish pattern is used to change an unwanted behavioral response to a particular stimulus or cue in the environment. Some people feel that they don't get as dramatic of a shift using the Swish pattern as other people report. We now know that, when the Swish is effective, what we are essentially doing is shifting internal eye dominance. Now we can shift eye dominance on purpose and make our work more precise and effective.

A: The Hemispheric Eye Model is ecological and safe because all of the information which leads to change is information within the explorer's own reality. **You are less likely to get resistance from people when the more effective response comes from making them conscious of what is in their unconscious mind.**

M: Al was curious about what was different about a Swish pattern process that resulted in the old behavior staying away and one in which the old behavior returned.

If you are taking an image from one eye, in essence one hemisphere, and it comes back into that same side of the brain, you may not actually have changed anything. If, however, you shift from one hemisphere to the other, the change will be automatic. With THE Model, the difference is already coded separately in each hemisphere, so the change is automatic and ecological.

Eric: I can see that the other mind's eye has an important role in phobia relief work too.

M: Right, and that is another reason we are having so much fun with this, especially in our client work. We have had instant success in shifting phobic responses to bees, spiders, heights, and in one case, flies.

A: We have been teaching just a small amount of THE Model with Core Transformation®. Core Transformation is a process that is going for the deep structure of an unwanted behavior or symptom. Core Transformation guides the explorer to a core state, which is a state of being, not of doing. If I am in my right internal eye, which accesses my left hemisphere (logical, linear thinking), and I am trying to access a state of being, I am not likely to be successful. If I can shift my attention so that I am in my left internal eye, which accesses my right hemisphere (spatial relationship), I will be able to connect more easily, and in an even richer way, to a state of being.

THE Model
for Learning and Memory

A: We are really excited about the possibilities in this next section. We will be discussing how THE Model has proven useful for memory. Marilyn is going to share with us a little about learning strategies, based partially on the NLP spelling strategy and partially on discoveries from Internal Dominant Eye Accessing. The work she has been doing with learning strategies in seminars, and in her private client practice, is *very* exciting.

There is an NLP presupposition that is appropriate for how we go about learning new things. **If what you are doing isn't working, do anything else.** In the past, one of the tools some school teachers used was to have a student correctly write a misspelled word one hundred times on the blackboard. This technique may have taught the student to spell one particular word, but it took a long time, gave the student writers cramp, (Laughter) and took away valuable time that the student could have spent learning other things.

M: Not to mention what social effects that technique had on the student, or the beliefs a student may have formed about themselves as a learner and as a person.

A: Fortunately, most people now recognize that there are more effective teaching methods than forced repetition.

The NLP Visual Memory strategy, which is often used to learn how to spell, is an excellent example of a simple and precise method of learning. THE Model adds to this already effective method.

M: As an example of how important hemispheric specialization is in a classroom setting, I will share something Al experienced during our early stages of discovery. He was experimenting with how to focus internally into a specific hemisphere. He is usually right eye dominant. When he shifted to be more left eye dominant, and tried to write something, he found he had trouble spelling.

A: The spelling went away, but my handwriting improved. When I was able to shift back to the more linear side of my brain, I looked at the word I had written a couple of different ways on top of a scratch pad, and both ways were spelled wrong. After I shifted back into my left hemisphere more dominantly, the way the word is actually spelled just popped in. My hemispheric dominance *did* make a difference. We will be discussing this more a little later in this section.

M: To begin the memory portion of this training, I would like to review the basic NLP spelling strategy. We learn new information in the three basic modalities: visual, auditory, and kinesthetic. The visual is what we see, both internally and externally; the auditory, is what we hear, once again internally and externally; and the kinesthetic, refers to our feelings. Due to the non-phonetic way words are spelled in the English language, using the auditory channel to spell can be very distracting and inefficient. For example, how do you spell the word "two, to, too?" Or how do you spell "right, rite, write?" (Marilyn writes the various spellings on the flip chart.)

In these examples, it is the context that makes a difference in how we spell the word. There are many other words that are not spelled phonetically, like the word "chauffeur." Even the word "phonetically" is not spelled phonetically. Phonetics has its place in reading, and when we need to know how to spell a word, a different strategy is required.

What is found to be common with excellent spellers is that they see the word in their mind's eye, and then get a positive feeling that the word is correctly spelled. If the word is misspelled in their mind's eye, the feeling they get is kind of a negative "yuck," which leads them to a back-up strategy, such as chunking the word down into sections or syllables or referring to a dictionary.

Another thing common to excellent spellers is that the auditory channel is quiet. Having their auditory channel quiet for the spelling strategy serves to eliminate negative or misleading internal dialogue.

People who are good spellers report that they have a visual screen, and the word just sort of "pops up" on the screen. When the word appears they are able to spell it forward or backward, and they can manipulate it to correct the spelling, if necessary. By understanding the key components of an efficient spelling strategy, we can teach the steps to people who want to spell better.

With my background of working with children in education, the strategy makes sense because it is very sequential and easy to understand. As a trainer, I taught this strategy for a couple of years. Yet, I had never seen an internal digital picture of a word. I would say to my clients, "Now look up to your left and make the word, and see the letters," and they would respond, "uh-huh, uh-huh." The spelling test results would improve, and they would get good grades and be very happy. I would think to myself, "I know this stuff works." I really believed in it, yet somehow it just wasn't translating in a way I could use for myself. Something was missing. Even having these specific steps available, I was still unable to process the information until Al discovered Internal Dominant Eye Accessing.

I had been attempting to visualize, and with practice I did get better. While driving, I would come up to a stop sign and look at the sign. Then, I would close my eyes and try to recreate the street sign in my mind's eye. I got so that I could create the word, one letter at a time. The first letter would come in. Then I would see the next letter, and the first letter would go away.

This is what often happens to children diagnosed with Attention Deficit Disorder. They report not being able to hold onto a picture, which can be very frustrating, because they are not able to control it.

In the past, if I were to talk to you about a movie I had seen, I would have seen an internal representation of the movie, often times in a metaphoric way, sometimes cartoonish, and sometimes with a sort of fluffy pink picture. I was able to see the image, but I couldn't see a printout of the words describing the image. I could see an image of a beautiful sunset in my mind's eye and have a sense of how it felt in my body. Even after I had practiced visualizing, I couldn't see the words "beautiful sunset." The digital words would not stay in my internal visual field. I really couldn't rely on my ability to do this process, even though I was successfully teaching others who wanted to learn to spell.

In working with shifting my internal eye, I discovered that I was only looking at a metaphoric picture. I was aware of my visual memory picture only while using my left internal eye, which was being directed from the right hemisphere of my brain. However, I wasn't using my right internal eye to access my left hemisphere in order to process the digital information.

I practiced by looking at the image of what I wanted to spell, let's say a tree, and then trying to spell "tree." Well, I know that I know how to spell "tree," so it wasn't so scary inside. I didn't have any of the emotional blocks from those old internal voices saying, "You can't do it right," or "You're not good enough," and so on. I could finally begin to see the word "tree," but it would still disappear on me. I just kept practicing and trying it, because it was working for other people.

A: Marilyn's comment about practicing reminds me of a quote I really like. It comes from Vince Lombardi, the great football coach. He said, "Practice doesn't make perfect; perfect practice makes perfect." The way Marilyn practiced makes more sense to me than making her write it on the blackboard one hundred times. (Laughter)

M: One morning, as I woke up, I saw our cat in the room. I looked up and saw an image of a cat in my mind's eye. Then, underneath the picture I saw these three little pink letters, "c-a-t," and I saw the letters with my other mind's eye! I could just feel which eye was doing the looking, and the minute I could see the cat's image with my left internal eye, the other image came up with my right internal eye, and it was "c-a-t." Then, I could see both the image and the letters simultaneously.

At first, when I tried to take the image of the cat away, the word "cat" would also go away. So for me, I needed to have a representation, or a metaphoric image of whatever it is that I wanted to remember, in order to get the digital or linear word.

A: Accessing both her left and right hemisphere by putting the image in her left internal eye, and the digital word in her right internal eye, holds the connection together for her.

M: I have finally learned a strategy that lets me hold the image and the word together.

Eric: So how do you know my name is Eric?

M: I recognize you and I have an auditory that says, "Eric." What I can do now is use the NLP strategy for remembering names. I see the person's digital name on their forehead and take a mental picture. I can actually do that now, because now I can see the image of Eric, and I can see "E-r-i-c." I can even see it well enough to spell it backwards, "c-i-r-E," which I could never have done before.

A: When we got a new cellular phone with a new phone number, I had Marilyn get a picture of the new phone in her left internal eye. After she accessed the picture of the phone, she shifted to her right internal eye and mentally typed the new phone number under the picture as I verbally said it to her. She was able instantly to memorize it that way.

M: I could see the number forwards and backwards. Being able to control my internal images in this way didn't happen for me the first time I tried it. If you have had difficulty getting pictures, I encourage you to stay with the Internal Dominant Eye Accessing process.

When we are learning something new, it often takes practice to be able to do it easily. I am evidence and proof, as are clients that I have worked with, that if we keep practicing we are effectively teaching our brains to *think* in a new way.

It is important to note that, when a child has a behavior pattern that does not fit comfortably into the classroom setting, sometimes a diagnosis of Attention Deficit Disorder is made. We find that in some cases it might be more of a learning strategy problem than an actual disability. In a classroom, when a more kinesthetic child is required to sit still, it is like telling them to stop thinking, because if they are not moving their brain isn't engaged. **There are many factors to be considered when diagnosing and treating ADD, and having an effective learning strategy is one of them.**

A: A friend and colleague has done a great deal of work using NLP technology in helping children diagnosed with Attention Deficit Disorder. He attended a presentation on Internal Dominant Eye Accessing at the NLP World Health Conference in Santa Cruz, California in 1997. After we had guided the group through an experience of shifting to the other internal eye, our friend reported that when he shifted eyes his pictures started jumping around and he couldn't control them. He said that it was similar to what his ADD (Attention Deficit Disorder) kids have reported about their internal images. Now he has a more empathetic understanding of the frustration they must be experiencing. It is interesting to note that our friend holds a Doctoral degree in education, so it is fairly obvious that he must have an effective learning strategy.

Ila: That's incredible! It goes along with a couple of the stories you have told about people who, when they saw an image with a different eye, it started jiggling and shaking. It's a great correlation.

M: If someone doesn't know that there is something better than images jiggling and shaking, of course sitting down and reading a book is going to be uncomfortable, and the information is not going to be assimilated.

Part of an effective learning strategy is being able to focus. Often, when we want to focus on something, there is external stimuli coming in. Normally, without even thinking about it, we say to ourselves, "Right now I want to take this piece of information and bring it into the foreground," and everything else just washes into the background. It is the way our brain automatically allows us to focus.

How many of you have had a sense of wanting to focus on something, and there is a lot of noise in the background, or there are ten other things you are thinking of? (Everyone in the group nods in agreement) Sometimes you can get really agitated with it and go into overload. You can imagine going through life that way and not being able to delete the external "stuff." Imagine the frustration of not being able to say, "OK, I just want to focus on this for now, and I'll take care of all those other things later." Think how uncomfortable that could be internally. As a result of being uncomfortable, children are not going to want to sit down and learn. This is another reason why being able to use both sides of the brain is so important. **Not only are we able to access visual memory, we can choose which hemisphere of our brain we go to visual memory with.**

Mike: Since you just said that, a question occurred to me in your example when you put the cat and the letters up in your visual field. Did you tell us that you used one internal mind's eye for the cat and the other internal mind's eye for the letters?

M: Right.

Mike: Wow, that's amazing.

M: And now it is becoming almost automatic for me, because I have been practicing the technique. Now my mind knows, "Oh, you want to use both hemispheres for this." Of course, there are many other people who just do that automatically.

Mike: How did you discover that the image of the cat, or any other image, and letters worked with different mind's eyes? Did you have one delete if you went to the other eye?

M: Yes. I would get a picture of whatever it was that someone asked me to spell, for example, "encyclopedia." OK, there's the picture of the encyclopedia. If you asked me to spell it, I wouldn't have a clue how from the picture I had. Even if I couldn't consciously see the picture, I could certainly describe the encyclopedia for you. No one ever said, "OK, now with the other eye, you can get the digital word, until Al taught me about my "other mind's eye."

A: The Hemispheric Eye Memory Strategy is simply a matter of holding the image from the right brain visualization, which is going to be the left internal eye, then shifting attention over into the right internal eye. This will add the digital word from the left hemisphere, connecting it to the image. Now the image and the digital word are in both hemispheres in the same picture, so they are hooked together. And as Marilyn said, some people do that automatically.

M: Most of us have had the experience that we can spell a particular word because we have seen the word externally in print. We have automatically put it into our visual memory where we can see it, and then we spell it.

How many of you have written down a word because you were not sure how it is spelled? You might write it two or three ways, and say to yourself, "That's the one I like, it feels right." It feels right because you have seen the word before, and there is a congruent match internally, even if it is at an unconscious level. If you have never seen the word before, or if you just don't know how to spell it, you need a back-up system. You can look it up in the dictionary or ask someone who knows how to spell it. Once you have an image of the word spelled correctly, you can put it in your personal data base of correctly spelled words.

It is important to be able to "see" what someone is saying because so much of our information comes in verbally, in school, in lectures, and from the boss. If we don't have a way to translate words into perceptual meaning, the information will more than likely just go away. It would be like trying to download a document from a Macintosh to an IBM without a translation program.

A method some people use to remember names is to make a metaphoric image or connection when hearing somebody's name. That method is similar to what we are doing. When we install the image and the name of the person in one picture, we will remember his face with his name connected to it. When we want to learn a new word and the definition, we see the digital word in our linear hemisphere and the metaphoric representation of what the word means in our relationship hemisphere. It is a personal choice as to whether the metaphoric image or the digital word is installed first. Either way will work.

A: It might take a little practice to determine which internal eye it is easier to access metaphoric images with, and which internal eye it is easier to access digital words with. Most people will access the metaphoric image from the left internal eye and the digital word from the right internal eye.

As we demonstrate to the group how to install a new word into both hemispheres, we will use the most common internal organization. If you are organized the opposite way, simply adjust to what works best for you. Somebody come up with a word that is challenging, but not too difficult, that we can use to demonstrate the process.

Linda: Desiccate.

M: OK, let's practice by having Linda spell the word for us and give us the definition, while we build it into our visual memory for both hemispheres.

Linda: Desiccate, d-e-s-i-c-c-a-t-e, which means to dry out, to remove moisture from something.

M: OK, you know now that "desiccate" means to dry something out, to remove moisture from something. Think of a metaphoric image that will give you that piece of information.

A: Now, using your left internal eye, visualize the metaphoric representation for drying something out or removing moisture from something. Once you have that image in your left internal eye, simply hold that image in your conscious awareness, then shift to your right internal eye and add the digital word "desiccate," d-e-s-i-c-c-a-t-e, to the image. Now you have the picture representing the definition and the digital word in the same picture.

Rita: I installed the word in syllables. I went de-sic-cate, and it worked.

A: Good. How you break up the word can also make a difference for some people. This is an excellent example of chunking a task into manageable size pieces.

M: We are accustomed to chunking in certain ways for syllables and telephone numbers. This technique is going to be easier if we use a method we are already comfortable with. Do it the way that works best for you.

A: I'll share how I installed the word "desiccate" into my memory. I got an image of a desert in my left internal eye, then I switched to my right internal eye and put the word up in red letters as "desi-ccate". I don't know why the letters are in red, but I trust that my unconscious knows. Now the image of the definition and the correctly spelled word are hooked together for a more complete memory.

Another way to chunk information is to separate it into a specific context. If I want to remember a telephone number, I will get an image of the person in the context of where that phone number will reach them. If it is their home phone, I might get a picture of them in front of a house. If it is their office number, I may see a picture of a building. Once I have that image in my left internal eye, I will shift over to my right internal eye and input the actual phone number. That way, instead of just having numbers, I have recall of numbers that mean something.

M: In summary, what we have found is, not only do we have a visual memory place for our eyes to access, but we also have the ability to use the right internal eye and the left internal eye together to have a more complete experience of a memory.

Having the conscious choice to install information into both hemispheres is having control over what previously seemed to be out of our control. If we have never learned to make words translate into images, the words simply don't have meaning, which then distracts from our ability to communicate. We might as well be reading French, German, or Hieroglyphics.

A: This same simple technique will also work for math skills, since visual recall is an effective strategy for memorizing equations.

Another exciting way to use The Hemispheric Eye Memory Strategy is in learning a new language. It is quite simple to remember words in a new language by connecting them with words that mean the same thing in our native language.

Let's go back to the example of "cat." The process stays the same, and when you get to the part of adding in the digital word, you also add the word in the new language. Suppose you are learning Spanish and you want to remember the Spanish word for cat, which is "gato." When you install the word in Spanish, you can simply add "g-a-t-o" underneath the word "cat" in a different color. You can use a different color for each language you learn.

M: An important part of an effective learning strategy is finding a way to bring both hemisphere's of the brain into our study of spelling, math, and languages. It is also important to consider a person's beliefs about themselves as a learner. Beginning with small successes, we can build up a pathway to explore what is possible and remove any perceived threat or negative judgment from failure.

Often in school, one of the biggest deterrents to an efficient learning environment is the threat of getting a bad grade, being yelled at, or being labeled as stupid. Children can get labeled as slow learners, not because they are unable to learn but because they haven't learned an effective strategy. Such labels have a way of directing students to form beliefs about themselves that they are not capable, therefore they must be worthless. There is also a good chance that they will give up on learning, even if at an unconscious level.

A: We look forward to this being a valuable tool for teaching children an effective way to comprehend and remember, thereby opening up new options for them to be life-long learners.

The Hemispheric Eye Memory Strategy

Purpose: To access left and right hemispheres of the brain to install information and recall for memory.

1. Establish rapport and ecology for working together. Calibrate the explorer for visual memory accessing. (See Chart D in Appendix)

2. Explain and demonstrate explorer's current external dominant eye. *This step shows that there is a difference in eye dominance and will assist in determining the internal dominant eye for The Hemispheric Eye Memory Strategy.*

3. Have the explorer choose a word (noun) that is easy to spell and that he already knows. We will use the example "cat." *This step is to learn the process and to create success.*

4. Have the explorer get a visual image of a cat using his left internal eye, and put this image in his visual recall field. *Usually located up and to the left for visual memory accessing.*

5. Say to the explorer, "Now allow that visual representation of a cat to remain here (*gesture to hold the image in the visual recall field*) as you shift to your right internal eye, and in a way that works for you, build in the letters 'c-a-t.' Now you are seeing the word 'cat' along with the picture of what a cat looks like."

6. Next, have the explorer choose a word he would like to be able to spell.

7. Build a visual representation of what the word means, using the left internal eye. Build the letters for the word with the right internal eye. (*Remember to chunk into small pieces, if needed*).

8. Repeat Steps 5 & 6 using an image of a person with his telephone number in the image.

9.   Test the explorer's memory of the easy word, the word the explorer chose, and the person with his telephone number.

10.   Discuss with the explorer when and where this process will be useful in his life.

A: Let's take a moment to review the handout for The Hemispheric Eye Memory Strategy. The intent of this process is to establish an effective method to remember a variety of things by installing information into both hemispheres. This is accomplished by starting out with a word that is easy to spell, in order to learn the process and to build in success. Then we move to a more challenging word that the explorer wants to learn to spell. The next step is connecting a telephone number with the image of the person that the number will reach. The purpose of this step is to build in success with memorizing a sequence of numbers.

Mike: Does it really help to project the image of the cat?

M: For me, it did.

Mike: Does it generally help, do you know?

A: My experience is yes. If we use Marilyn as an example, it seems obvious that she was trying to build linear information into her visual recall while accessing the portion of her brain that is more concerned with metaphoric images.

There is another important distinction that plays a role in how to install facts into the visual recall area using the eye accessing model. (See Chart D in Appendix)

When people do an internal search for information, there is a tendency to move their eyes to the locations described in the eye accessing model.

When you ask someone an easy question, like how to spell her name, she usually looks straight ahead, and answers quickly. It's when she has to search for the information that she begins moving her eyes to specific locations in an attempt to create or remember.

Physically, our eyes are set in our heads at an inward angle, which allows us to have a point of focus that is directed toward the center of our visual field. (See Chart B in Appendix) With this physical arrangement, it is easier to look to the left of our visual field using our right eye, and easier to look to the right of our visual field using our left eye.

Since the motor responses for the right side of the body originate, and are directed from, the left hemisphere, a right eye focus tends to access information stored in the linear left hemisphere, which is where words and familiar information are stored. When our eyes go to the left, it is physically easier to use our right eye.

When our eyes go to the right, it is physically easier to use our left eye, which is accessing the right hemisphere. The right hemisphere tends to be more creative and is also where unfamiliar information is processed.

We found that, using Marilyn's situation as an example, when she was looking up and to her left to install a word into memory, she was going so far to the left that it became more difficult to use her right eye to focus. If a person looks far enough to the left, his nose can actually block the visual pathway between the right eye and where he is looking. Of course, the same physical scenario holds true while accessing to the right side.

We have consistently had more success helping clients build information into the visual recall field when we have had them access visual recall just slightly to the left of center.

Marilyn was accessing her left eye (right hemisphere), while looking up and to her left. The shift in her being able to use the memory strategy effectively came when she was able to access her right eye, while looking up to her left, which gave her more access to her left hemisphere.

You can do the memory strategy simply by switching internal eyes, which directs the brain to the appropriate hemisphere for the task at hand. Even though the memory strategy can be used effectively by shifting internal eyes, we use the eye accessing portion of the NLP Spelling Strategy because it works.

In NLP literature, eye accessing cues are explained as being "hardwired" in the neurology. Moving one foot at a time to walk is also naturally hardwired, because it is easier and more effective than moving both feet at the same time. It is also naturally easier to access a specific hemisphere, consciously or unconsciously, by directing the location of the eyes. (Chart D in Appendix)

We have shared this perception with several people who are familiar with eye accessing cues. When we do, one question that consistently comes up is, "Why do we access up for visual, middle for auditory, and down for feelings?"

As we look down, it tends to pull us into a posture with our shoulders forward and our head moving down slightly. Our breathing also slows down and moves lower into the abdomen. When we notice these physical cues in people, we are alerted to the possibility that they might be depressed. One of the things we can offer someone in a state of depression is to have the person look up. We even hear it in metaphoric language when people start getting out of a depression. They say, "Things are *looking up*." Their physiology changes and their mood shifts, at least to some extent.

With the physiology of looking down, there is also a sense of turning inward. This explains how we go into auditory digital (internal dialogue or self-talk) by looking down and to the left and into feelings and emotions by looking down and to the right. We hear it in metaphoric language when someone says, "I'm *downright* mad."

Looking down and to the left uses the right internal eye which accesses words in the left hemisphere. Looking down and to the right uses the left internal eye and accesses the emotions related to identity issues and spatial relationships, which are located more in the right hemisphere.

When we access auditory, we are looking toward our ears where sound enters our perceptual awareness. Again, recall is to the left, and construct is to the right.

When we move our eyes up to access visually, there are two things that play a role. The first is the reverse of the physiology of looking down. The second is that there is usually less external input, or clutter and distraction, above the center of our visual field.

Most people who access visually prefer large open spaces when thinking or learning. For example, if I have my computer facing a wall, I don't think as well as when it faces an open area, with my back to the wall. If I'm facing a wall, I don't have a place to make pictures, because the wall is in the way.

Most external sensory stimuli occurs at eye level or below, so it makes sense to look away from clutter to a more open space for visual access. This may be done either consciously, or out of conscious awareness. Eye accessing is more precise as a calibration and strategy tool when we understand how it works in the brain.

Remember, we think and give names in one hemisphere of the brain, and we experience and give meaning to life in the other hemisphere.

M: For me, it is like having both sides of my brain in rapport with each other. Rather than trying to turn off a part of my brain to concentrate, I am allowing the metaphor side of my brain to do its job, while inviting the linear side to add to my experience.

A: We want new information to be programmed into the visual, auditory, and kinesthetic systems in each hemisphere as much as possible. The more representational systems we put information in, the more representational systems we have to trigger recall when the information will be useful. What we are learning here today is how to consciously input information into each hemisphere.

Gail: So, we should make the cat meow.

A: Why not? And, if you are learning a new language, you could have the cat meow with an accent. (Laughter) It does add the auditory channel to the memory. Another effective way to add the auditory is to say the word out loud, especially if you are learning a new language.

Tim: Marilyn, you said that you were not using the other eye for memory. Is that a matter of the information actually being in your mind but out of conscious awareness, and then bringing it in?

M: Yes. It had to be there, because I am a literate person. I can spell and write term papers, and I made it through college. I did rely on spell check a lot, and I did that thing called reversing (referring to dyslexia). I would reverse the letters and even the words at times. On one level I had the capability. It's just that I didn't have the internal processing strategy to do it on purpose, and to do it precisely.

A: There is a quote that comes to mind which goes along with Tim's question. It's from Dr. Barbara Brown, from the department of Psychiatry at UCLA Medical Center. She said, **"If a person could see something of himself that up to now had been unknown and involuntary, he could identify with it and somehow learn to exert control over it."** This is what Internal Dominant Eye Accessing allows us to do. Our brains have all the information and capabilities we need. Now we have one more way to access the brain's potential, and to use that potential to direct us toward new heights.

Loosening a Stuck State

A: When doing personal and professional change work, our goal is to get from being "stuck" in a negative state of mind or situation to a desired outcome. The way to make the shift happen is by adding resources to the stuck state to enable the transition to happen.

Stuck state + Resources = Desired state

First, so we will all have the same understanding, let's define, "What is a stuck state?"   Another way to perceive this is as a challenge.   For our purposes here, we will define "being stuck" as an emotional state or a situation in which movement to another resource state or behavior *seems* out of reach.   Often we are unconsciously blocked from change by a hidden positive intention, or there is a secondary gain for one or more parts of our self.

Often times, getting to a desired state is difficult because we have not "let go" of whatever has been keeping us stuck.   During times of draught, aboriginal tribes living in the Kalahari Desert in southern Africa are able to find water because baboons are unwilling or unable to "let go."

Baboons are very intelligent animals and, because of their keen sense of smell, they always know where to find water. They are very secretive about where the water source is during a draught, and will not go to the water when any other creature, including man, can follow them. The aboriginal tribes-people use an ingenious method to entice the baboons to reveal where there is water. Rock salt is a rare commodity in the Kalahari. Since baboons need it to survive, they will consume large amounts of the salt when it is available. The tribes-people leave an enticing trail of small pieces of the rock salt leading to a large anthill. Anthills in the Kalahari are tall, solid structures with small holes in the exterior just large enough for the baboon to put a hand into. The tribes-people put a handful of salt into the hole, then hide and wait for a baboon to take the bait. When the baboon gets to the anthill and reaches into the hole with the rock salt in it, the baboon grabs as much as it can fit into its hand. Of course, with its hand full of salt, the baboon can't remove its hand from the hole. Once the baboon is "stuck" to the anthill, the tribes-people can leisurely approach and slip a rope around the baboons neck. After releasing the baboon's grip on the salt, the tribes-people give the baboon more salt to eat. After eating its fill of salt, the baboon gets so thirsty that it ignores the secrecy of the water source and leads the tribes-people right to it. It's interesting to notice that the baboon's refusal to "let go" is what ultimately causes it to be manipulated and captured.

If the challenge or stuck state didn't have some power, chances are we would not be stuck there in the first place. Even when the desired state seems to be more compelling than the place where we are challenged, we can remain stuck simply because we are more accustomed to what is familiar. Once we are successful in loosening the challenge state, it becomes easier to establish the desired state as the more comfortable choice.

Sometimes, loosening the grip of a stuck state is simply a matter of having a choice about our initial internal response to a stimulus. There are five things that need to be in place in order to move from a challenge state to a desired state.

First of all, there has to be recognition that there is a problem. If we don't know that we are stuck, there is no motivation to change. We are probably not going to change behaviors or emotional states until we recognize there are options. Just guiding clients in the direction of realizing that they have choices about how they feel or react is a big step on the way to their having what they really want.

Then second, there has to be a desire to change. A desire to change begins with a motivating influence that moves people away from pain or toward pleasure.

Third is a well-formed outcome. This helps us know specifically which direction to point the brain. By having a well-formed outcome, we are able to see if the change is something we really want to have. It is also important to consider how making the change will affect friends, family, and co-workers. (See appendix for conditions of a Well-formed Outcome)

The fourth requirement is having a process, technique, or strategy to elicit the change. The Hemispheric Eye Model enhances the effectiveness of any process, technique, or strategy.

The fifth requirement for change is an integral part of the other four, and is so important that it also stands alone. The fifth requirement to loosen a stuck or challenge state is safety. **Ironically, without a perception of safety, no change is likely to take place. Yet often it is the very issue of being safe that dictates the necessity for change.**

Chris: That's what I feel like today. I feel so much more centered. I have had a very old pattern of falling into "I'm not OK, there's something wrong with me." It's something I have been working on for a long time. This work with the internal eye seems to be the straw that made the difference in being open to change.

Last night I went to an event that didn't turn out to be what I had expected, and I felt like I didn't want to be there. The experience was different because I didn't fall into my old pattern of thinking, "Oh, it must be me." I didn't find myself blaming somebody else for the way I was feeling. I simply decided I didn't want to be there, and I was very clear about being free to do what I wanted to do, so I left.

I know it was this process that made a really huge difference in my being OK to just do what I wanted, even though it seems kind of scary to have the new emotions that go along with the change.

A: What I find interesting in Chris's statement is that she now has a choice over what she feels, therefore she has control about what she wants to do.

I did The Hemispheric Eye Foreground-Background process with someone who had a close friend who had been injured in an accident. When we got to the step where she had the choice of having her initial internal response be the image with either more or less emotions connected with it, she chose the one that had more emotions. She recognized that her feelings were appropriate for the experience and intended to honor those feelings of sadness.

What Chris is sharing is similar in that she recognized her old pattern and had the courage to do something different. Whatever shifts are taking place for Chris are probably because of the new information and choices that she is experiencing from the work we did yesterday. To Chris I would like to say, "I salute your internal wisdom." It is this kind of courage that makes change possible.

M: Sometimes stepping into that place of change where things are new, and perhaps sad or scary, can seem like being in an airplane that starts dropping because it hits an air pocket. The feeling can be one of, "I don't know if it's going to stop before I hit the ground, or not." You can either panic, or ride it out. Sooner or later you will find that there *is* a bottom to that air pocket.

A major key to change work is giving ourselves permission to have our feelings. It also takes a high degree of trust that if we are not in a place where change is ecological, there will be a part of us that protects us from attempting that change.

A: This is similar to what we were talking about yesterday. Already inside of our brain, there is important information in both the left and right hemispheres. A lot of times we get stuck more dominantly in one side or the other. If we are stuck in our emotion and relationship side without the facts, we are using only a part of the information that is available to us. If, on the other hand, we get stuck in the linear side, we are likely to go through life without actually feeling it. This doesn't make much sense to my way of thinking! By having conscious access to both sides of our brain, we have more choice in all situations.

M: As a consultant, gathering information that may be out of a client's conscious awareness is extremely important for change work. This is why THE Model is a valuable addition when aligning *perceptual positions.* Perceptual position is the term used to describe three viewpoints present in any interaction. The first of the three perceptual positions is called *self,* which is seeing through our own eyes, being fully associated, and feeling our own feelings. The second perceptual position is *other.* The *other* position is having a sense that we are in the position of the other person we are interacting with, seeing the situation from their viewpoint, and getting a sense of what they might be experiencing. The third position is the *observer.* The observer is a viewpoint positioned to watch equally the two individuals involved in the interaction. This position is neutral (dissociated) and has no emotions about the interaction. The observer position is for gathering sensory based information about the specific behaviors and reactions of the people involved. It is often compared to having the viewpoint of a movie camera.

By checking both internal eyes from each perceptual position, we are able to gather more precise information from self, other, and observer.

We don't always want to be a clinical observer, even though sometimes it is appropriate. I worked with a client to help her align her perceptual positions. When she was in the observer position, there were emotions that really belonged to the self position. We were able to give the feelings back to her self position, and when she stepped back into self, she didn't know how to deal with the feelings. With her new perspective, we were then able to create behaviors that allowed her to have appropriate and useful personal boundaries.

Sometimes anger, frustration, and sadness are really wonderful signals for us to take appropriate action. If we recognize those emotions as signals, they are sort of like a fire alarm. A fire alarm is useful to signal us that there might be some sort of danger. Yet, if we depend on the fire alarm to put out the fire, we could be in deep trouble. When an alarm goes off we need to take action to keep ourselves safe, put out the fire, or, in some cases, discover it was just a false alarm.

We want to be able to use the signal of an emotion to take conscious and appropriate action, to say: "OK, what do I need to do to be safe here?" "How do I need to react or respond?" "What is the truth about the situation from a standpoint of current reality, rather than a possible miscalculation or a projection from the past?"

A: Victor Frankel said something that I really like. He said, **"Suffering, which is an emotion, ceases to be suffering when we come to fully understand it."** I think that what is happening for Chris is that she is now accessing the information from her unconscious resources that will lead to the understanding of the emotions.

M: Occasionally, when I work with people, part of the issue is that they don't want to feel their feelings. They just want to come in and do a quick fix. In some circles, NLP has been misrepresented as being just a quick fix of the surface structure stuff. If you only deal with an issue at the surface level, it is like saying, "Just take it away, I don't want to feel it," instead of really being able to say, "What is underneath those feelings that needs to be resourced, healed, or shifted." Then the task becomes finding the positive intention of our behaviors and the beliefs that are supporting those positive intentions, so that we can make the appropriate adjustments.

If there has been a history of dysfunction, abuse, or other negative events, we might think, "It's not safe to feel, it hurts too much, and I don't want to go there anymore." A more effective way to respond is to realize that we do have resources and emotions are sometimes just signals that it's time for change to happen.

Joyfulness and happiness are signals that what we are doing is really wonderful. Let's find out how we are getting the good emotions, so we can learn to experience these more often. We are always working toward creating a safe place from which to experience our emotions.

Jay: I think I am experiencing some of what Chris is. I think it has a lot to do with what Marilyn just talked about. When I think about the deep-seated issues that I have worked on for several years, sometimes there is terror from thinking there might not be a bottom. I have worked on stuff around a certain issue, but thought that if I ever really hit this one on the head, I would just fall forever. I have been doing a lot of introspective work, and now I think that there *is* a safe way to work on this issue. As deep, and potentially painful, as I sense the issue is, I can see now that I can at least contemplate changing, instead of running the same pattern of avoidance again.

A: This is a little bit of what we talked about yesterday with a phobia or a trauma. If, when we think about a traumatic event, the image is right in front of us as a three-dimensional, color movie, in stereo, are we likely to work on the issue? If, however, we can simply switch internal eyes and the picture moves away, taking the panic feelings with it, it can give us the internal safety required to do the kind of healing that will make a permanent difference. When the image changes, we are literally able to see the event from a different perspective.

M: How many of you have ever gone back to an experience from childhood, and found it was really different than what you remembered? You look at it and think, "You know, when I was a kid that was much bigger," or, "Gosh it seemed like it was just huge when I was younger and now it's just this little thing."

I remember going to visit a place every year during the summer when I was a child. We visited one of my Mom's best friends, who lived on a ranch. She had a huge reservoir with a cement bottom that was used as a swimming pool. I remember diving in, and it went forever to the bottom. Years later, I had the chance to go back to the ranch, this time taking my two sons. I had been telling them, "You'll love this, because you'll get to dive and play in this huge, deep, cement reservoir." When we got there, I found that "forever to the bottom" was actually about six feet deep. (Laughter) Looking at it with my adult eyes, it was just this little, tiny, round pond.

If we do this in our mind with other events that were hurtful as a child, and look from the child's perspective, it seems like, "I don't want to touch that emotion, it's huge, it's too scary." We put it away and leave it in that hugeness that seems so unsafe. Looking back at an issue or event as an adult, with the perspective of current reality we have today, the issue might not be so big. Maybe it has shrunk. Maybe it's only six feet deep instead of "forever to the bottom." It becomes a matter of recognizing that we have a lot more wisdom and resources now than we did at those times. **Emotional healing begins when we can look at a past event and say, "What is the truth about that?"**

Larry: Last night I did an interesting Foreground-Background process with a friend. The main difference was that in the first picture they felt out of control, and in the second picture they were still real angry, but felt more in control.

M: The feeling of being in control can be a wonderful resource to have. A lot of times in seminars people work on issues involving a co-worker, a spouse, or a child. After the participant makes personal changes during the seminar, they report back later, "That person really changed." Of course, it was the person in the seminar who changed the interactive loop with the other person. When one part of a system changes, it requires the other pieces of the system to change at some level.

In the example of "still being angry and being in more control," your friend is likely to begin setting more well-defined boundaries, and the anger can still serve the purpose of keeping them aware that those boundaries are important.

Getting What You Want

A: Have you ever noticed when you hope for something, that sometimes it doesn't happen and other times it does? On the other hand, when you expect something to happen, it seems to happen more frequently. We would like to have you get into groups to explore what is going on in your internal processing for things that you hope for and for things that you expect.

First, think about something you *expect* to happen, and notice how you represent that expectation internally. Notice the visual, both internal and external auditory, and the kinesthetics. Next, think of something you *hope* will happen, and repeat the process of checking out how you represent that internally. Take a moment to notice what differences there are between what you hope for and what you expect. We will regroup to see what similarities there are between your individual processing and what others in the group experience.

(The group breaks and returns)

M: What did you discover?

Rita: Hope was a big picture, in the future, and fluffy. For hope, people in our group seemed to look up into their visual field. For expect, they seemed to access kinesthetically down and to their right.

M: Alright, who else?

Ila: Hope was warm, colorful, and dissociated. The picture for expect was black and white, with substantial detail, and associated.

Carol: I did it with my personal life and with my professional life. With both hope and expect, my personal life was muddled and unclear and my professional life was more solid.

A: For your personal life "muddled" and professionally "more solid." Could you say more?

Carol: Sure. My personal life was vague and wishy-washy, "Maybe I will, and maybe I won't." In my professional life it was step-by-step, like when I got my masters degree and other successes I've had.

Sean: Hope is in the future sometime and expect is now, or at least soon. Also, in our group, when people talked about hope the words were fluffy, and the voices were softer and had more rhythm. When we talked about what we expected, the voice tone was more matter of fact.

Dori: For me, hope was *way* out into the future, while expect was within a week. As I think back now, I notice that hope was dissociated and expect was associated.

Larry: In hope, there were pieces missing from the picture. It didn't have everything I needed. With expect, the picture was clear, clean, and all the pieces were there.

Dori: My picture of hope was more flexible and generalized. Expect was more detailed.

Susan: The school where I work had a meeting to discuss our hopes and dreams. They asked us what we wanted the school to look like ten years from now. The first thing I thought was, "I might not even be here ten years from now, so I don't even want to think about it." They asked us, "If you had a million dollars for the school, what would you want?"

A: I hope you asked for a really nice employee lounge and highly paid teachers. (Laughter)

Susan: That's a good idea. I hope they ask again when they really have the money. As soon as they say "if," it doesn't seem possible. I don't want to waste my time dreaming, in case there are any strings attached.

Don: The voice tone of my internal dialogue was really different. For hope, it was dreamy and said, "Wouldn't that be nice?" For the thing I expected, my internal voice sounded certain and said, "Yeah, this is going to happen!"

Jay: I wonder if it's what we are accultured to. We are taught that, when we hope for something it might not happen, and we will be disappointed and feel bad. I know some people who think that it's not OK to hope for something, but it is OK to plan for something.

A: That seems to go along with some of the examples where hope is fluffy, and expect has more detail. It is an excellent point that we often get accultured to perceptual filters that may not serve us as well as would other filters.

A concept used in change work, that I find very interesting, is being able to identify useful beliefs and limiting beliefs, then having the opportunity to adopt the most useful beliefs available as a replacement for existing limiting beliefs.

How many of you noticed more than one picture for something they hoped for? (Several participants raise their hands.) Right. When identifying limiting beliefs, our focus is directed toward how language influences our internal experiences. One example is telling a child "Don't spill your milk." What usually happens when we say that? Right, the milk gets spilled. The reason this happens is because the unconscious mind deletes the word "don't," and creates an experience of spilling the milk. In a sense, when we say, "Don't spill your milk", we are actively manifesting what we "don't" want to have happen. We tell the child's unconscious mind, "Spill your milk." A more serious context is telling someone, "Don't do drugs," or, "Don't drink and drive."

The dictionary defines "expect" as: *regard as likely; assume as a future event or occurrence.* "Hope" is defined as: *expectation and desire combined.* Notice that, with hope, there are two possibilities, what we expect to have happen and what we desire to have happen. If we hope for something, we are actually getting two representations. One is of getting what we want, and the other is a counter example of not getting it.

What we are suggesting here is that, if we notice that there are two representations of something we want, it is to our advantage to recognize what information is in the counter example that can be useful.

It is similar to "Murphy's Law" which states, "Whatever can go wrong, will go wrong." Most people with whom I have discussed "Murphy's Law" consider the statement to be that of someone with a negative or defeatist attitude. As I understand the origination of the statement, it is actually a statement that leads to manifestation.

Murphy was one of the engineers on the rocket-sled experiments to test human acceleration tolerances that were done by the United States Air Force in 1949. One experiment involved a set of 16 accelerometers mounted on different parts of the subject's body. There were two ways each sensor could be glued to its mount. During the connection of the mounts, somebody had managed to install all 16 mounts the wrong way. Murphy's pronouncement regarding the inevitability of the mishap then spread to other technical fields connected to aerospace engineering. It was intended as a check and balance strategy. Since nobody knew exactly what to expect while sending a rocket into space, aerospace engineers wanted to cover all unseen possibilities. This way, if it were possible for something to go wrong, alterations to the design, function, or process could be implemented prior to completion of the project. It is a way of increasing the odds of success by acting on, and controlling, the external world to the best of our internal ability.

The first time new parents go out to dinner, they call a babysitter they think they can trust, make sure there is food for the baby and the sitter, and make sure the babysitter knows how to lock the doors. They will probably give the babysitter the phone numbers of a relative, a neighbor, and the restaurant where they will be dining. They might even call home somewhere between their salad and their dessert, just to be sure things are alright at home.

By taking all these precautions, the parents are doing what the aerospace engineers were attempting to do, which is to do all they can in order to have as much control over external events as possible. The more specific their attention to detail, the more successful their efforts are going to be. As the couple is preparing to go to dinner, they are thinking of all the things that might be needed in their absence. They are hoping that things will be OK while they are gone, and they don't leave until they expect that everything has been taken care of.

By paying attention to information that is in our pictures of what we hope for, we can begin to manifest our desires by eliciting as much control of the external world as possible.

I have a great example of how this process works in reverse. When I was an assistant golf professional, I often played golf with the head professional, a cagey veteran who had an excellent way of introducing the concept of "expect to hope" to his opponents.

In golf, it is important to focus on the middle of the fairway, where you want to hit the ball. The sixteenth hole at my home course had a lake that ran most of the way down the left side of the fairway. As his group stepped up to the tee, the head professional would look out at the lake and say, "Boy, there sure are a lot of ducks on the lake this afternoon." Even though his opponents may have been aware that he was directing their attention to the lake on purpose, the statement still had the desired effect of adding the lake into their awareness, therefore causing them to lose full attention on the middle of the fairway.

My experience was that people hit more balls into the lake when he brought it into their awareness than when he didn't. I would like to point out that this was done in fun. It is a good example of how we may be sabotaging our hopes by having either conscious or unconscious options about what we want in life.

M: I always hoped to go to Switzerland. Then I realized I wasn't taking any action to make it happen. When I shifted to manifesting the trip, I got a passport and started to find out some of the places that I will go when I get there. Now that I am taking action toward my outcome, it feels different inside.

Ila: For my internal dialogue the words were different. For the things I hope for I kept getting reasons why I can't, so I was concentrating on "Why not?" When I finally found something I expect, my words went to "How to."

A: Notice the second representation for what Ila hopes for, the auditory that says, "Why not?" It is also interesting to notice that, for Ila, hope seems to be more reactive, while expect sounds more proactive.

Gail: If I hope for something, a second thought that comes is, "Maybe not."

A: Once again, a second possibility shows up.

Eric: Hope is like a luxury, "Wouldn't that be nice?" Expect is procedure, "That's just the way it is."

M: I worked with a client who was hoping to be a famous actress some day. Her picture was beautiful; there she was on stage winning awards. Since she wasn't getting any acting jobs, I asked her, "What do you see when you are going to an audition?" She saw herself not getting the job. Her expectation was of not getting the part, so she manifested what she expected to have happen in a negative way. For some people hope feels better, and hope is nice to have in our lives. Sometimes we forget the "how to" of making the dream happen.

Chris: When I expect it, there is no question about it, I just know it. Things I hope for seem to depend on someone or something else.

Stan: I hope to have a million dollars, so I bought a lottery ticket. (Laughter) If it's important enough to me to have the million dollars, I need to find a way to make it that is more in my control.

A: Somebody is going to win the lottery, which is an example that sometimes what we hope for does happen. Sometimes the external world jumps up and "lets us have it" in a good way. There are, however, many more examples of people who have a million dollars because they took the steps within their control to make it happen. Notice how well Stan qualified his statement by saying, "If it's important enough to have."

Dreams are wonderful, and what we are exploring here is how we can have more control over making those dreams come true. If our dreams are too big and fluffy to begin with, we can start to make our dreams come true by "chunking" the dream into manageable size pieces.

An example of chunking is, suppose it's time to clean the house and the task is overwhelming because so many things need to be done. The size of the task may keep us from beginning. If we chunk the task down into manageable size pieces, we might begin by starting with one load of laundry then going to the kitchen and cleaning it. Even cleaning the kitchen can be chunked down into separate tasks of dishes, the counter top, and mopping the floor. Once an outcome has been identified and approached in manageable sized chunks, the chances of having our outcome increases. If we use the chunking strategy for manifesting our dreams, we greatly enhance our chances of having them come true, so please keep dreaming.

M: It is similar to the Walt Disney Strategy for creativity. You can start with any dream, then create a plan through the filter of a realist, then evaluate the plan in order to make the dream come true. By cycling through the filters of dreamer, realist, and evaluator, amazing things can happen.

Tim: When I hope for something, I get fear from what I expect to have happen.

M: When we expect the negative, it can keep us from realizing our dreams or hopes. The negative possibilities contaminate what we are allowed to hope for.

Tim: I used the example of a date I have tonight, and was hoping to have an interesting evening. When I thought about it, I remembered a lot of other dates I had in the past that were really boring. As soon as I got all those pictures of the boring dates, I found that I also expected tonight's date to go that way.

A: So this is a good opportunity to chunk down to find out what is setting these dates up to be boring. Have you ever had a date that was not boring?

Tim: Oh yeah, lots of them.

A: Good, now you can begin to discover what the external components are which are out of your control, and what components you *are* in control of, in order to manifest an interesting date. My guess is that you are now going to have more internal resources that will lead you toward influencing a positive outcome. When we change ourselves, it will also change the rest of the systems in which we are interacting.

M: Of course, our intent is never to control another person. By being the best we can be internally, we are more likely to elicit the best responses another person has to offer. The action of expecting and acting as our most resourceful selves is something that *is* in our control.

A: Thank you all for your input and examples. We have a basic list of how some people represent the difference between what they hope will happen, and what they expect to have happen, that we will pass out now. It is also a flow chart of the sequencing for going from hope, to expect, to manifesting your dreams.

The important thing to remember here is that there is a difference in our internal representation of something we hope for and something we expect. As with so many things in life, the differences will vary to some extent between individuals. By recognizing the differences that are unique to you, you can begin to elicit control in turning your dreams into reality. We invite you to use this handout as a guide to chart your own personal representation.

When we hope for something, and we get a "Yeah but" or any other secondary representation internally, it is our internal signal that there is more information to consider, or that there is some form of internal conflict about having whatever it is that we hope for.

When we get an image of what we want to manifest, we can shift internal eyes to find out what other information we already have coded inside our brain that will assist us in our manifestation. Of equal value is accessing our other mind's eye to check for any unconscious information that might prevent us from being fully congruent in our quest.

Hope to Expect = Manifesting

Hope	Expect
Right brain - Dream	Left brain - Fact
Maybe	Just is
Has counter example; "Yeah, But"	Congruent
External influence	Self directed
Reactive	Proactive
Imprints from Past, projected to Future	Current reality
Limiting beliefs	Flexibility

Flow from: Hope
                       ↓
- Internal Dominant Eye Accessing
- Well-formed Outcome
- Aligned Perceptual Positions
- Neurological Levels Aligned
- Beliefs in Current Reality

                       ↓
Flow to: Expect

                       ↓

Result: **Manifesting in Reality**

We have already discussed the different cognitive styles of the hemispheres. The right hemisphere is more involved during the processing of unfamiliar information. Once the information becomes familiar, the left hemisphere becomes more responsible for it. Referring back to Maxwell Maltz's theory, it takes twenty-one days for a new behavior to become a habit. After the information becomes familiar and is transferred over to the left hemisphere, it becomes expect or "just is."

Even when what we hope for meets the other criteria of ecology and chunk size, we still need to be congruent with our outcome in both hemispheres. We even hear it in our language patterns. For example, how many times do we hear someone say, "I have half a mind to...." (Laughter) A more effective way to accomplish our goals would be to have a "full mind" to.

Another common phrase is, "On the other hand...." When someone is talking about beliefs or goals, they often demonstrate, "On the other hand...," with their gestures by saying something like, "I really want to start exercising (gesturing with their left hand), but I don't have enough time. As they begin to say "But I don't have enough time," the left hand drops to their side, and they begin to gesture with the right hand.

In this example, since the motor responses for the left side of the body originate in the right hemisphere, the first statement, "I really want to start exercising," is coming from the right hemisphere. At that point, the familiar information in the left hemisphere says: "No you don't. I have historical evidence that you don't exercise." This is when the hand gestures shift to the right hand because the motor responses for the right side of the body are controlled by the left hemisphere. In essence, the left hemisphere doesn't believe the right hemisphere. This indicates internal conflict at some level. Half of the mind believes one thing, while the other half either has doubts or believes something else. When you see someone gesturing symmetrically with both hands while making a statement, it is an indication that they are congruent in both hemispheres of their brain.

Note to reader:

As an example that people can manifest their dreams, Marilyn traveled to Switzerland before this book went to print.

A Roadmap to Health

A: In order to have our resources working for us, we need to have all of the information stored in our neurology in alignment. The first step is to recognize when there is a conflict. This can be done by finding what information is in our unconscious mind by accessing our other internal eye.

One of the most powerful resources for change is found in our personal belief systems. There is a great deal of evidence that a limiting belief will sabotage almost any endeavor. This is especially true in the healing of serious illness. Although many factors are involved, a commonality to be considered is that patients who have healed from cancer had a belief that they would heal. It does not make any sense to me to think that all a cancer patient has to do to return to good health is to believe that they will heal. Many other things should be taken into consideration, such as diet, medical treatments, exercise, lifestyle changes, and overall self-image. If all those who have healed from cancer had a belief they would heal, it *does* make sense to me to have that belief in place.

This brings me to visualization techniques being used to access a person's natural healing abilities. One of the visualizations that has helped cancer patients elicit their bodies' natural healing abilities is to visualize sheep grazing. Metaphorically this represents the white corpuscles eating the diseased cells. The human body is a naturally healing system, and this is a wonderful way to let the body know what you want it to do.

A question that came to me was, "What is the difference between a cancer patient who uses this visualization technique and heals, and a patient who uses the same technique and does not heal?" One possible answer lies in hemispheric congruence or incongruence. For those patients who healed, was the belief that they would heal, in both sides of the brain? For those who did not heal, the belief may have only been in one hemisphere, and a *sequential incongruence* occurred out of their conscious awareness. If the message is sent to the immune system by only one hemisphere, only half of the patient's resources are being used. For those who have the belief that they will heal in both hemispheres, a *simultaneous congruence* occurs.

Hypothetically, suppose a person goes to his doctor for a check up and the doctor finds cancer. At that point most people are already set up for disaster, because in our culture we tend to hear that when someone gets cancer, they die. Even though now there are many examples of healing from cancer, the focus is often directed towards the not healing examples.

Since many types of cancer occur later in life, many people who are diagnosed with the disease grew up at time when cancer was regarded as fatal. The medical community was not then as successful in the early detection and treatment of the disease as it is now. The old beliefs about cancer, however, may still be firmly planted in the left hemisphere, where information seems to be matter of fact. If this is the case for someone using visualization techniques in their healing, there may be unconscious sabotage when the new healing information becomes a victim of the sequential incongruence pattern. It is easier to elicit a healthy outcome when there is a simultaneous congruence in which the beliefs about healing in the right hemisphere are accepted as fact in the left hemisphere.

Consider how this would apply to a people who want to stop smoking. If in the right hemisphere they get an image of themselves without the behavior of smoking, then almost instantly, the left hemisphere responds, "Oh yes you do, I have evidence." The left hemisphere is responding to the prior evidence in which smoking was a known behavior. As in the example of healing from cancer there are other considerations; however, even when those other considerations are taken care of, if the matter of simultaneous congruence is not addressed, there will be a degree of internal conflict toward the desired outcome. **Once we become simultaneously congruent, our desired outcome becomes, "Just is."**

It is important to understand what is so important about being able to visualize in personal well-being. Visualization is one of the oldest forms of healing. Science is now beginning to understand some of the reasons behind the success of positive visualizations. In the previous section, we learned about going from hope, to expect, to manifesting an outcome. We have explored how visualizing can be used as an effective strategy for change, and how important Internal Dominant Eye Accessing is to effective visualization. **Effective strategies only work when they match physiological functions.**

The fact that the human body has the ability to self correct from disease, and to adjust for changes in the environment, is becoming more obvious as we learn more about the intricate workings of the connection between mind and body. An example of this is that when the external temperature drops we begin to shiver, which raises the body temperature. On the other hand, if the temperature in the environment rises we perspire, which causes evaporation on our skin to cool us down.

Just going through daily routines there are many external visuals to which our bodies react, from the stress response of seeing flashing red lights coming up behind us on the freeway to the calmness and security of recognizing an old and trusted friend. Being able to respond appropriately to information from the external world keeps us safe.

The stress response is useful in preparing us to react to danger. There are three basic areas that will initiate the stress response. The first is in response to danger, either real or perceived. The second is change, whether we consider the change to be positive or negative. The third situation that will cause the stress response is internal conflict. Any one of these three potential triggers for stress can be initiated by what we see, either externally or in our mind's eye. Nightmares and flashbacks are examples of how our mind's-eye can produce physiological responses to what we see.

The experiments Pavlov did with dogs demonstrate another example of external stimuli creating physiological responses. After a bell was repeatedly rung prior to feeding, the dogs became conditioned to responding to the bell by salivating. Of course, it wasn't the bell that caused the dogs to salivate, it was the anticipation of the food that would come after the bell.

Further research has shown that the anticipation of the effects of drugs will actually begin to activate those effects physiologically. When people first start taking heroine, they experience the drug state with a relatively low dose. As they continue taking heroin, more of the drug is required to elicit the same level of "high," because of the blocking of receptors in the brain where that particular drug attaches. Eventually, in order to get the same effect from the drug, drug users need to take a dosage that could be lethal to someone taking the drug for the first time.

If a heroine addict has established a pattern of going to a friend's house to take the drug, his friend's house becomes part of the external stimuli that prepares his system for the effects of the drug, similar to Pavlov's bell preparing his dogs for food. If the heroine user breaks the routine, prior to taking the drug, in a way that disrupts or alters the external cues that the drug is on the way, his body won't be able to prepare for the dosage it is about to receive. If, for example, he chooses to take his heroine at his own apartment, and his body doesn't have warning that the drug is on its way, the same dosage he regularly takes at his friend's house may be lethal to his unprepared system.

Another excellent example of how the body automatically adjusts to an external stimulus occurs when people regularly take a drug that increases their heart rate. The anticipation of taking the drug will cause the heart rate to slow down so that when the drug speeds up the heart, the heart rate will stay within a safe range.

Knowing that we *do* respond internally to what we see, hear, and feel, it makes sense to have our internal images match what we want to have. **If we want to be a happy, healthy person, and we have an internal image that represents that outcome, our physiology will respond accordingly.**

Note to reader:

I highly recommend the book <u>Beliefs: Pathways to Health and Well-being</u> by Dilts, Hallbom, and Smith, for further insights on the influence beliefs have on our health.

Having More Than "Half a Mind" to Change

A: Understanding how important it is to have a well-defined self-image, we are going to move on to building a compelling self-image for a specific behavior. This exercise is designed to help us identify what information we have coded in each hemisphere and begin integrating that information toward a specific outcome. **This process will take a statement such as, "I have half a mind to exercise," into, "I have a full mind to exercise."**

Often, when we want to accomplish something, we simply don't have all the information required to be successful available to our conscious awareness. This process will uncover what has previously been out of our awareness in a way that lets us know what needs to be in place to make a desired change. Once all of the necessary information becomes conscious, this process integrates the information to form a condition of simultaneous congruence.

The NLP presupposition that says, **"People already have all the resources they need,"** applies here. As I begin to guide someone through this process, it is important for me to remember this presupposition. And I have found that people *do* have the resources. My goal in this process is to help the explorer become more aware of what she already know at some level.

This process will work for any behavioral change that you want, but maybe you keep putting off, or coming up with excuses why you don't change.

I would like to demonstrate "Creating a Compelling Self-Image for a Specific Quality or Behavior." I am looking for a volunteer who has "half a mind" to do something, or has something that they haven't gotten around to doing yet.

Ila: Will it work for losing weight?

A: Sure, come on up. Just a comment as Ila is on her way up. It is always important to notice the ecology in a statement of what someone wants. If we listen to the language of the statement and notice how it may be pointing the brain to an outcome, we may notice that losing weight in and of itself may not be ecological.

M: Notice how the phrase "losing weight" may take us somewhere we really don't want to go. A couple of months ago, I weighed myself and shared with Al that I had lost two pounds. He asked me, "What would happen if you lost your purse?" I answered, "I'd try to get it back." Knowing that once the two pounds are gone, I don't want them back, we now have a new way of phrasing it. Now I say, "I've released two more pounds back to the universe." There are plenty of children in the world who can use the two pounds once I have released them.

(Al takes a moment to establish rapport with Ila and to make sure she is comfortable in front of the group.)

A: OK Ila, thanks for being willing to share with us. So just to check out what you would like, is it about losing weight, or is it about releasing weight in a healthy way?

Ila: Oh, it is definitely about health, and losing weight is a part of being healthy.

A: Is it about releasing weight in a healthy way, and only to the point that you can maintain your ideal weight?

Ila: Right.

A: OK, in your mind's eye, go ahead and get the image of you that is healthy, at the appropriate weight.

Ila: OK, I've got it.

A: Where are you seeing that image?

Ila: It's just right out here. (Ila gestures out about fifteen inches, and slightly to her left.)

A: OK, now, it's helpful if I know where you are seeing the image. For the other submodalities, the most important thing is that you are aware of them. What I will do is have you notice certain qualities of the image that seem to be useful. It's OK for you to notice any others that I don't happen to mention. If you want to comment on any of them as we go, that's alright too, or you can just notice them.

Ila: OK.

A: Good. First I would like you to notice the visual components of the image. Notice if it is color or black and white. If it is color, notice the qualities of the color, and if it is black and white, notice the degree of contrast.

Ila: It's color.

A: Now check to see if it's a movie or a still picture, the size of the image, and if it's framed or panoramic.

(Brief pause)

Ila: OK.

A: Now see if there is anything besides the image of you in the picture. Take a moment to become aware of more specific information in the image, like your hair, your face, and maybe even your clothing. Check what your body looks like in this image, the shape and the body posture. Just let me know when you have had a chance to pay attention to those things. (Another brief pause, and Ila nods yes.)

Now check if there are any external sounds as you look at that image.

Ila: External sounds?

A: Either coming from the you in that image or from the environment around the image.

Ila: No, no sounds, it's just quiet.

A: How about internal sounds? Listen for any internal dialogue or any other sounds as you look at that image.

Ila: I'm just seeing somebody that looks happier.

A: So, it's an evaluation of being happy. How about feelings inside your body?

Ila: It's an overall feeling of well-being all around me. (Ila gestures with both hands around her mid-section.)

A: Is that a feeling just around your mid-section?

Ila: No, it's all over.

A: OK, check inside your body. Is there a more specific feeling inside as you look at this image?

Ila: Yes.

A: Where do you feel that?

Ila: In my knees and in my legs. For me, my intent is to keep the weight off my knees, because I know the extra weight puts extra pressure on them.

A: What does it feel like in your knees and legs as you see that image of you?

Ila: There's more energy and more bounce.

A: Now, I'm guessing, so just to check it out with you, is it more strength?

Ila: Yes.

A: So there is more energy and bounce that comes from feeling more strength in your knees and legs. Good. What is the age of the healthy you with the appropriate weight you are seeing in that image?

Ila: I guess I'm looking at me the last time I was that weight, which was when I was about thirty years old.

A: OK, now get a sense, which eye are you seeing this image with?

Ila: My right.

A: Now that we have the information from this picture, we can set it aside for a moment. In a way that works for you, I would like you to now get the image of what the healthy you at the appropriate weight looks like through your left internal eye. Let me know when you have that image.

Ila: (Brief pause) OK.

A: Tell me a little bit about that picture.

Ila: It's right out here. (Ila gestures to a spot slightly to the right of the first image.)

A: What size is that picture?

Ila: It's approximately the same size.

A: When you say approximately the same size, it leads me to think it's a little different. How is it different?

Ila: A little smaller, and it isn't as focused. It's a little fuzzy.

A: Less focused and fuzzy. Is it color or black and white?

Ila: Still color.

A: Still in color. Notice the quality of the color.

Ila: Not quite as bright as the other, but still bright.

A: Once again, become aware of the visual components of this image. Notice body shape, your face, and maybe even what you are wearing. (Brief pause) Notice if there is anything other than the image of you in this picture. (Brief pause as Ila checks out the picture) Are there any external sounds in this image?

Ila: No, it's quiet.

A: How about internal sounds or dialogue?

Ila: No, there doesn't seem to be any.

A: So now, go ahead and, as you are seeing this picture of the healthy you through your left internal eye, turn your attention toward the inside of your body for any feelings associated to this image.

Ila: I'm feeling it in my legs again.

A: And it feels like?

Ila: There's a heaviness there.

A: Alright, interesting. So as you are looking at this image, is there an evaluation word for what you see here?

Ila: Do you mean like a judgment?

A: It could be a judgment, or it might just be a word that represents what you are noticing. (Pause) Is there any emotion or evaluation attached when you see this image?

Ila: There's happiness.

A: OK, now checking this image, how old are you in this picture?

Ila: Now.

A.   Now. So this image is at your current age?

Ila: Yes.

A: I'm curious, what is the shape of your body in this picture?

Ila: The way it is now, but with a view to trimming it down.

A: So, is it like a beginning point of an action?

Ila: Yes.

A: Good, so what we are going to do now is have access to both images at the same time. It's like being co-conscious of the information from each image. Can you put them both out there so that you can see them at the same time?

Ila: Sure.

A: OK, good. Since we know that there is valuable information in each of these images, we are going to label one of them as the compelling image and the other as the resource image.

   The compelling image is whichever image seems more compelling to you. Then we will bring the information from the resource image over and add it to the compelling image, so that eventually we will have all the information that is valuable for this issue represented in a single perception or image of you.

So as you look at both images of the healthy you at the appropriate weight, which of those would you like to be the compelling image, and which would you like to be the resource image?

Ila: The first one is more compelling.

A: OK, the first image, the one with your right eye, we will call the compelling image, and the second one, from your left eye, will be the resource image.

Ila: Because the resource image is my age now, I will be able to use all I have learned up until now, right?

A: That makes sense. What I would like you to do now is to notice what skills, feelings, or qualities are in the resource image that would be valuable to the compelling image.

Ila: There is a lot of value, if I will use it.

A: You are exactly right, it represents all that you have learned. What we are looking for here is to be able to identify the specific learnings from that part of your brain so we can add these resources to the information that is already in the compelling image. Once all the information is together, you can begin using both sides of your brain consciously to achieve your outcome.

What are some of those qualities in that resource image? If you were to begin by just picking one of those things you have learned, what would that be?

Ila: Exercise is one of the most valuable.

A: So in the resource picture, you recognize the value of exercise to maintain good health. It may also involve having the resources to exercise, like having exercise equipment and knowing how to schedule opportunities to exercise.

Ila: I know the feeling of the strength I will have from exercising.

A: Good. So take the knowledge of the benefit of having strength from the exercise, and bring it over and incorporate it into the compelling image.

Ila: OK.

A: Notice how the compelling image changes with that resource added to it

Ila: It feels even better.

A: It feels better, and how do you notice that it feels better?

Ila: Well, I'm noticing it in my legs, which have been my big problem area.

A: Now we have one valuable piece of information added to the compelling image. Checking back to the resource image, what other skills, resources, or feelings will be nice to have over in the compelling image?

Ila: Eating better. That picture seems to have more knowledge about the proper types of food to eat.

A: So the resource image knows what types of food to eat?

Ila: Well, it's learning what types.

A: Which makes sense, because it is an ongoing thing, and there is enough information there to already be of value to the healthy you.

Ila: Right.

A: So in a way that is right for you, allow that knowledge to come over and join into the compelling image. Notice now how that compelling image changes. What change do you notice this time?

Ila: Feeling, a feeling of lightness.

A: Take just a moment to feel the lightness. Good, now I am guessing there is other important information in the resource image. As we bring more things over to the compelling side, just notice how the compelling image changes as those resources are added.

Looking back now at that resource image, what other skills, resources, learnings, or feeling are in that image that will be useful to the compelling image of the healthy you?

Ila: Expectations, commitment.

A: Is it expectations of commitment?

Ila: No, it's both.

A: Alright, so expectations and commitment. Somewhere inside of you, you know what having those resources is like. Sometimes, it is a feeling inside, and some people like to bring things that they feel on the inside, and just let those feelings flow into the compelling image. So now, in a way that is right for you, add expectations and commitment into the compelling image of the healthy you.

Ila: (Pause) I have an overall feeling of well-being.

A: Great. Take a moment to enjoy that overall feeling of well-being. (brief pause) When you are ready, check back with that resource image. Notice, are there any other resources, learnings, skills, or even feelings that will be of value to the compelling image of the healthy you?

Ila: There is a big desire to have health.

A: Alright, so there is a big desire to have health. You already know how to bring that big desire over and add it to the compelling image, so as you are ready, go ahead, and take all the time you need. Just let me know when you have done that. Notice how having a big desire for health enriches the compelling image of you.

(At this point of the demonstration, Ila's breathing has become fuller and the color in her face has smoothed out. Her speaking voice has become slower and deeper. This indicates that there has been a significant shift in her physiological responses as she looks at the compelling image.)

After you have taken a moment to enjoy this feeling, check back to the resource image. Are there any other resources, skills, qualities, or feelings that will be valuable to that compelling image?

Ila: I can't think of any more.

A: OK, so now what we have is this compelling image of the healthy you at the appropriate weight. It has desire, and a feeling of overall well-being that comes from expectation and commitment. It also has lightness and the knowledge of what kinds of foods to eat. There is the value of exercising and the strength you will feel in your legs. It is an ongoing process, and it is happening, along with all those learnings and awarnesses that were already in the compelling image. Notice how having all that information from the resource image added to the compelling image makes it more real.

Ila: Yes, it really does.

A: Good, how has the compelling image changed now?

Ila: Visually I don't notice much of a change, but emotionally, great change.

A: You discovered some valuable information from the resource image that had a lot of feelings attached.

Ila: Yeah.

A: Since this is the visual representation of the healthy you at the appropriate weight, we want to make sure it is a life-size image. Is the compelling image this tall? (Al holds his hand out to indicate Ila's height.)

Ila: OK, it already is.

A: Great. I would like you to be able to receive a message from the compelling image of you. So, simply step out of where we are now, and let's go over and have you stand in your compelling image and face back at the you standing back there with Al at the seminar. (Ila steps ahead into the space where she was seeing the compelling image, and turns to face the spot she had been standing.) As you step into this compelling image, you can go ahead and breathe into the feelings of lightness and strength, and just allow those feelings to flow throughout your entire body. (Pause while Ila integrates this information.)

That's right, now being the healthy you, is there a message of encouragement to send back to the you who is just one step away from being this compelling you? You can share it out loud, or it might be a private message just for her. Either way is alright. So in your mind, just deliver that message, taking all the time you need.

Ila: (Ila nods yes.) OK.

A: Watch her receive the message, noticing her response and acceptance as she receives it.

Ila: (Brief pause) OK. (Ila nods yes)

A: Alright, let's step back out of this image now and
back into the you who is in the seminar with Al doing this
process. (Al and Ila go back to their original positions.)

OK, we are back here now, and the compelling you
just one more step into your future has a message for you.
So from here, go ahead and receive that message as she
delivers it.

Ila: (Brief pause as Ila listens to the message. Ila smiles
and nods yes.) OK.

A: What we are going to do now is make sure that the
new, more resourceful, compelling self-image stays in
both hemispheres of your brain. This is the image that
began in your right internal eye, so I would like you to
hold the image as it is, with all the feelings, and shift
internal eyes to see it as it is now with your left internal
eye.

Ila: (Ila nods yes.) OK.

A: Alright, now check back with your right eye, and
then back to your left eye, to make sure the image and
feelings are the same in each eye.

(Brief pause)

Ila: OK, it's the same.

A: Great. Now here's the fun part. Step into this fully
integrated image of the healthy you at the appropriate
weight. (Ila takes one step forward) As you do, breathe
into the feelings of lightness, strength, and overall well-
being. Take a moment to enjoy the feelings, knowing that
this all comes from what you already know to be true

about yourself. It's all information that came directly from you.

(Brief pause)

Ila: I like it. It feels natural.

A: Good. When you think about you now, maybe tonight or tomorrow, what things will be different? What will you be doing differently?

Ila: I will be goal oriented and committed. I'm going to be doing it.

A: Good, so what is an example of doing it?

Ila: Well, for example, when I go to lunch today, even though in the past I have tried to be conscious of what I eat, now I will be more dedicated to it. As far as exercise, I see me doing more of it by taking more opportunity when I have the time.

A: It is also nice to remember that you can continue to breathe into these feelings of being healthy any time you want to feel good. You might even recognize the qualities of this image each time you see your reflection in the future.

(Al thanks Ila for doing the process as a demonstration for the group, and she returns to her seat.)

Any questions about the process?

Larry: How many more times would you have to do that process with her to make a change?

A: Let's ask her. Ila how many more times do you think you need to do the process in order to have a change?

Ila: I feel like it's already there. It's just done.

A: I think Ila's response answers the question better than I could. I have a belief that change doesn't take time, it takes commitment. It is commitment that takes time. **Once the commitment is made, change is instantaneous. What this process does is bring the information together to speed up the commitment time.**

Gail: Do you ever erase part of the self-image?

A: No, we are not looking to take anything away. What we *are* doing is adding options and choices by accessing information from each side of the brain. To have a useful balance, we need to have the information from each hemisphere blended together. For example, if you want the water to be warm when you wash your hands, you need some hot water, and some cold. When you mix them together you can adjust the temperature to be more comfortable. The same type of thing is happening with the information in the left and right hemispheres. Instead of erasing part of an image, it is more useful to identify what the learnings are from the image. Sometimes the resource image directs our attention to lessons we have learned, and sometimes it cautions us about what to avoid in order to achieve an outcome.

M: It is interesting what happens sometimes as people begin to bring resources from one image to the other. For some people, the resource image stays the same. For others, each time they bring over a quality, feeling, or skill to the compelling image, it deletes from the resource image. When the resource image dissolves, they can tell that all the qualities have been added to the compelling image.

A: Sometimes, there will be a feeling or belief carrying enough weight, that, when it is added to the compelling image, it brings the rest of the resource image over with it.

Note to reader:

As of this printing, Ila has released 38 pounds back to the Universe, and her cholesterol level has lowered 80 points. She exercises regularly and continues to be fully congruent in her desire to be healthy at the appropriate weight.

Creating a Compelling Self-Image in Current Reality

A: The demonstration with Ila is an example of creating a compelling self-image for a specific behavior.   The next step in our workshop is to build a compelling overall self-image.   Building a compelling self-image for a specific quality or behavior will have an effect on our overall self-image.   Sometimes it is valuable to have a self-image that is pervasive throughout every aspect of our lives.

When I feel good, it seems to me that the attendant at the gas station is in a good mood, the waitresses are pleasant, and the other drivers on the freeway are courteous.   It seems to be more where I am coming from internally than what is going on in the external world that makes the difference.   It is the self-image that I am stepping into that creates the perceptual filter I respond from.

We are going to have you get with a partner and first just elicit your partner's current self-image.   Some useful questions to elicit a persons self-image are, "How do you see yourself?" and, "If you were to describe your self-image, what do you see?"   As guide, you are going to help the explorer notice how he is currently representing himself internally, and then note the specifics of his submodalities described in the handout that says "Current

Self–Image." At this point we only want you to assist each other in identifying your current self-image. We will do more with it later.

M: The way we are going to ask you to elicit the current self-image is by following the same basic format you did yesterday, when you elicited submodalities for The Hemispheric Eye Foreground-Background Process, with one additional step. This time, we want you to get the age of the person as they are in their self-image for each eye.

M: After you have elicited the current self-image, I would like you to say, "So, notice which internal eye you are seeing this image in more dominantly." After you get that information say: "Now I would like you to shift to the other internal eye. As you do, notice what your self-image is with your other internal eye."

We will have another set of internal visual, auditory, kinesthetic, and emotional representations from the other internal eye. We are only gathering information to find out what the perception of the self-image is at this time. This exercise is designed to give us a starting point from which we can develop a compelling self-image.

Don: Do we do both internal eyes now?

M: Yes, we will do both internal eyes now and use a separate form for each eye.

A: Elicit the submodalities from the first image that you get, and find out which internal eye that image is in. Then elicit the submodalities from the other internal eye.

Stan: What do you do if someone is having trouble switching to the other internal eye?

Current Self-Image

Question:

"What is the internal image you currently have of yourself?" or, **"When you think of yourself, what do you see?"**

Information to gather:

Visual – Size; Location (*gesture to where you see the image*); Color or Black and White; Brightness; Full-body or Part; Posture; Movie or Still; Framed or Panoramic; Height.

_____

_____

Auditory – How does your voice sound?; Tone; Tempo; Volume; What does your voice say? or, What do you say about yourself?

_____

_____

Kinesthetic – How do you feel about yourself? Notice any physical feelings in your body.

_____

_____

Emotions or Evaluations –

_____

_____

Age of the self in the image: _____
Internal eye you are seeing the image with: _____

M: What I have found that works really well is to say
       something like, "Just allow your unconscious mind...."
       If it is taking a moment, or you get a response like, "Well,
       there's nothing there," say, "Well, just stay with what you
       have so far, and let your unconscious mind continue to
       search for the image."

       For people who, in the past, have not had much
       success in recognizing their internal pictures, it might
       take just a little time and patience to allow them to begin
       accessing the images. Even for people who access their
       internal pictures easily, it might take a little time to shift
       from one eye to the other, since this is a new concept to
       the conscious mind.

A: Sometimes people who have had difficulty seeing
       pictures begin to develop their natural ability to visualize
       simply by shifting to the other internal eye.

Chris: Do you need to say self-image or can we say self-
       esteem or self-concept?

M: We like to use the term self-image rather than self-
       esteem or self-concept, because we know how much our
       pictures influence us even if they are totally out of our
       conscious awareness. Using the term *self-image* directs
       us to that portion of our brain that has more access to the
       visual system. We have all heard that old saying, "A
       picture is worth a thousand words." Actually, it takes
       most people at least seven minutes to read those one
       thousand words, and it would take many more words to
       describe what is in most pictures. So, even though some
       of us may prefer the kinesthetic or auditory system,
       myself included, I know that pictures and colors are very
       impactful. I purposely use the term self-image, because it
       is the whole concept of self, rather than just a theoretical
       talking about self. It's more of the Gestalt self.

OK, if there are no questions, choose a partner. It shouldn't take more than about ten minutes each way.

(Group breaks for the exercise and returns)

M: Who would be willing to share what they discovered about themselves? Yes, Don.

Don: Well, Chris was eliciting from me, and the first stuff that came up was through my left internal eye. What was really funny was I wasn't sure which eye I was seeing it with, so I covered my left eye with my hand, and all of a sudden--no more picture. I covered my right eye, and the picture was still there. I figured, well, I must be looking through my left internal eye.

M: Good way to calibrate, right? In fact, some people do find it easier to access their internal eye by covering one of their external eyes. It seems to set an example for the unconscious mind as to what you want to have happen internally.

Don: In my feeling about that picture, there was a lot of sadness, melancholy, and emptiness. The picture was probably eight or nine feet away from me, and it wasn't really pleasant to look at. I probably don't need to recap the whole process, but when Chris said, "So, now notice what it's like when you look at a representation of yourself through your other internal eye," I just let whatever was in the other eye come up. The content changed, submodalities changed, and I saw this picture of me with considerably more detail, and it was about this close. (Don gestures about fifteen to eighteen inches in front of him.) I almost couldn't see anything except me in the picture, and there was a lot more color in my face.

In the picture, there was a different sense of the way I was breathing that was much deeper, more relaxed, and fuller. I could just barely look through and see past the area between my ear and my neck in the second picture, from my right internal eye, and there was a very deep blue background behind the image. I don't know if there is any significance to the blue background or not. I also had a sense that my arms were out and welcoming, in an embracing kind of way. My feelings about this picture were entirely different. It felt really good.

M: That's wonderful Don. Tell me, do you have a sense of your age in either of the images?

Don: Same.

M: Both current age?

Don: Yes.

M: Good. This is another question that we have found very interesting. Sometimes when you elicit the age of the person as they are in the image, they are not current age, and often it is a different age in each picture. Thank you for sharing your experience with us, Don. There is definitely a significant difference between the two internal senses of self in your example.

Who else would be willing to share? Yes, Jay.

Jay: When you mentioned age, I realized that age was one of the things that came through for me. I had two really different experiences. In the first one, the picture was of me at my current age, although the beard kind of comes and goes, obviously it's not part of my self-image. In the other internal eye, the picture was very indistinct. It was a sequence of short clips of myself at much younger ages. There was also an interesting reversal of which channel various feelings were coming in through when I shifted eyes. (Other channels here refers to the modalities of Visual, Auditory, and Kinesthetic.) When I see the picture of myself at my current age, my internal evaluations are very positive, but there is an auditory track that runs through it which is quite critical.

M: So, the auditory is incongruent with the picture?

Jay: Yes. It is incongruent with the picture, and the overall emotion is one of despair, depression, anger, and frustration.

M: In the auditory, Jay, do you notice if the voice is saying "I," or is it saying "you?"

Jay: The voice is saying "I." They are "I statements," and it seems to be my own voice. When I went to the other internal eye, although I didn't see the pictures clearly, because they seem to be very amorphous and changing quite rapidly, my evaluation of the picture is negative, whereas my voice tone is very matter of fact. I am simply listing who I am. "I'm Jay, I play keyboards, I'm a martial artist," and so on. Even the things that should have an emotional quality to them, like "I'm married," are simply listed or stated predominantly as fact.

M: And which eye was that with?

Jay: With my right eye.

M: So again, quite different perceptions from one internal eye to the other. Can I share a little bit about your experience Sean?

Sean: Sure.

M: At first, Sean was bogged down in the image of *what* he does, rather than an image of *who* he is. He is in a career change right now, going from working with what he has done for a long time into more of a retirement, a joyful kind of place where he really wants to be. He was stuck with thinking of himself as his activity. What we do is certainly a facet of who we are, although it is only a small part of our identity.

In our sense of self-image, being stuck in that "doing" sense can be very limiting. It is a lot of the reason why when people retire, or their job is eliminated, and they are forced into a "doing" change, they lose a sense of self. Their identity is enmeshed with what they "do" more than with "who they are." They don't tap into the deeper structure of understanding that the "doing" part of them is just a manifestation of the "being" part of them.

When I go to the deeper structure of myself, I know that my mission and passion are teaching, and there are many ways I can teach. I see myself as someone who shares knowledge, and helps others through my teaching. When Sean switched internal eyes, he had a deeper sense of himself that was not attached to his activities. He started to tap in a little more to the quality of Sean as an essence.

A: At this point, there are two important things to notice. The first is that quite often there are very different perceptions in each hemisphere. The second is that there is valuable information in each perception. The desired outcome from having this awareness is to incorporate the information from each perception into a compelling self-image. What we see, both internally and externally, is extremely important to how we experience life.

As a guide, I have the presupposition that there is value in the images from both hemispheres. Sometimes, when we do this process, the explorer is sure that there is nothing in one of the images that would be of benefit. If we have the belief that even such negatively perceived emotions as fear and anger serve a purpose, we can begin to find value in all the information that is available for a specific issue. Fear serves as a warning of impending danger, anger signals a violation of our boundaries, and loneliness might simply bring to our awareness the value of being with other people.

The built-in ecology of this process is that all the information comes from the explorer. As guide, I only want to suggest some options as to what the value might be, if the explorer sees only negative. **It is important to remember that the explorer is the authority on their perceptions.** With this in mind, remember to be gentle as you suggest options of what might be valuable.

In the demonstration with Ila, the image she accessed in each internal eye was an image of herself, one at a younger age, and one at her current age. This happens quite often. One client got one image at current age, and the other image at age thirteen. When I asked him to identify one image as the resource image, and the other as a compelling image, he chose the one at age thirteen to be the compelling image. As we began adding in resources, the compelling image of him began to age. By the time he had added in all the resources, the image had become current age. **If we trust the explorer to know himself better than we do, things will work out.**

There are two situations when neither image can be determined as compelling. One is when the explorer has a negative internal response from each image, to the extent that he is uncomfortable identifying either one of them as compelling.

M: The first image that came up for a woman I worked with was the image of her mother. The second image was of her when she was six years old, which for her was a very unhappy time of her life. In her case, neither image was compelling, or even close to current reality.

A: The other situation is when both images are metaphoric, such as a butterfly in one eye and an oak tree in the other. Each will represent aspects of the person, and will contain valuable information, yet neither is of the person. Since we want to have the self-image be current reality and compelling, we have found the following technique to be effective.

A hologram is basically a three dimensional image. If neither image is compelling, have the person identify three or four personal qualities that are verifiably true. Next, ask her what she looks like with those qualities or truths. Sometimes it is easier to start with height, hair color, and other physical features.

Next I ask the explorer to identify some positive qualities she knows to be true, or that family or friends would say about her. I have her get a holographic image of herself with the physical features and qualities that she knows to be true.

Next we identify the images from both internal eyes as resource images. We then begin to add the resources from both images into the holographic self-image. Sometimes the explorer will choose to bring in all the resources from one image before bringing in the resources from the second image. Other times, the explorer chooses to add resources by alternating between the two images.

There are two similar processes for creating a compelling self-image, so we are going to give you two handouts, one for each process. One is for a compelling self-image for a specific quality or behavior, which we demonstrated with Ila. The other process is for an overall compelling self-image. Although you can use a holographic image for either process, we have not found it to be necessary for working with a specific quality or behavior.

Creating a Compelling Self-Image for Specific Behavioral Change

Purpose: To create a self-image that enhances a specific quality or behavior using information from both the left and right hemispheres of the brain.

1. Establish rapport and ecology for working together, and elicit what quality or behavior the explorer would like to *be different.*

2. Guide asks, **"What would the you look like that** *(backtrack what the explorer wants to be different)***?"** *Elicit submodalities and which internal eye the explorer is "seeing" the image with.*

3. Guide says, **"Now, have a sense of you with this desired quality or behavior with your other internal eye. (Pause) Notice what is different in the second picture."**

4. Guide says, **"Now that you have access to both pictures, get a sense, or simply notice, which picture**

is more compelling?" *(Identify one image as the compelling image and the other as the resource image.)*

5.   Guide asks, **"What information, skill, resource, quality, or feeling is in the resource picture that will enhance and enrich the image of the compelling you?"**

6.   Guide says, **"In a way that is just right for you, bring that *(backtrack resource)* over now to become a part of the compelling image."**

7.   Guide says, **"Notice how having *(backtrack resource)* changes the compelling image of you."**

8.   Guide asks, **"What other...?"** *(Repeat steps 5, 6, & 7 until all appropriate information has been added to the compelling image.)*

9.   Guide has the explorer integrate the compelling self-image into both hemispheres by seeing the compelling image identically through each internal eye.

10.   Guide directs the explorer to associate fully into the compelling image by saying: **"Now, I want you to step forward into this compelling image of you. Experience being fully and completely the resourceful you."** Guide says, **"Breathe into the you now that has *(recap qualities)*. Turn and face the current you, and send a message of encouragement from this compelling you."**

11.　　Guide has the explorer step back into the current self and receive the message of encouragement from the fully integrated compelling self-image.

12.　　Test and future pace in several contexts what the explorer will be doing with the new behavior.

Creating a Compelling Self-Image in Current Reality

Purpose:　To create or enhance a congruent and compelling self-image using information from both the left and right hemispheres of the brain.

1.　　Establish rapport and ecology for working together

2.　　Guide asks, **"When you think of you now, what image do you see?"** *Elicit submodality distinctions and which internal eye the explorer is seeing the image with.* Guide then asks, **"How old are you in this image?"**

3.　　Guide says, **"Now in a way that is just right for you, get an image of you with your other internal eye."** *Elicit the differences in submodalities.* Guide then asks, **"How old are you in this image?"**

Note:　If neither image is compelling, or if neither image is of the person, (two images of someone else or two metaphors) have the explorer create a hologram consisting of what they physically look like with some of the positive qualities they know to be true about themselves. If a hologram is required it becomes the compelling image, and the two original images *both* become resource images. If a hologram is used, continue the process with step 5.

4. Guide says, **"Now that you have access to both images, get a sense, or simply notice, which image is more compelling."** *Guide allows the explorer to select one image to label as the compelling image and to label the other image as the resource image.*

5. Guide says, **"What information, skills, qualities, resources, or feelings are in the resource image that will enhance and enrich the compelling image?"**

6. Guide says: **"In a way that is just right for you, bring (_backtrack resource_) into the compelling image. Notice how having (_backtrack resource_) changes the compelling image."**

7. Guide asks, **"What other...?"** Repeat steps 5 & 6 until all appropriate information has been added to the compelling image.

   Note: Not all information needs to be added to the compelling image. Always allow the explorer to determine what information is ecological to add.

8. Guide has the explorer integrate the compelling self-image into both hemispheres by seeing the compelling image identically through each internal eye.

9.   Guide directs the explorer to associate fully into the compelling image by saying: **"Now, I want you to step forward into this compelling image of you. Experience being fully and completely the resourceful you. Breathe into the you now that has** (*recap qualities*)**. Turn and face the current you, and send a message of encouragement from this compelling you."**

10.   Guide has the explorer step back into current self and receive the message of encouragement from the fully integrated compelling self-image.

11.   Guide future paces how the explorer's life will be different with the new self-image, and what new behaviors the explorer will have in the future.
Option: Suggest that the explorer notice this self-image each time the explorer looks in a mirror.

A: OK, if there are no questions, get with your partner and create some compelling self-images.

(Group breaks to do the exercise and returns.)

M: We saw some wonderful integrations, and since this process connects at such a deep level, rather than talking about it, we will let your experiences stay personal and allow you to keep integrating as we continue.

A: We have covered a lot of information, and now you have an understanding of the concepts and some of the processes of Internal Dominant Eye Accessing.   We would like to take a few moments to share some examples of how we have been using this model, and how you can begin to take this information out into the world.

The first story is an example of how shifting internal eyes can make an instant perceptual change that defuses a stress response.

We introduced The Hemispheric Eye Foreground-Background Process to a group in Argentina.   One of the women at the training went home that evening and used the process with her husband.   She reported that, when she got home, her husband's heart was palpitating as he thought about the pressures he was having at work.   She had him think about the situation using his other internal eye.   His heart immediately slowed down, he took a deep breath, and relaxed.   He said, "That's better, I'll take care of it tomorrow."

His problems at work didn't go away, but after the process he was able to be in a more resourceful state to deal with whatever was going on.   His experience is similar to what I have learned to do on the freeway when someone cuts in front of me, or when the traffic is exceptionally heavy.

Simply seeing a situation from a different perspective will often be enough of a resource to help us feel empowered and be in control of our emotions.

Another example I would like to share involved a client who had been working through a serious health issue.   He had already had the appropriate medical procedures and was healing at a rate that surprised his physicians. His presenting issue was experiencing panic from thinking, "What if something goes wrong?" It is easy to understand the positive intent of a part that wants everything to be OK physically. Yet the physiological responses that were a part of the panic state were causing an unnecessary strain on the very organs that had required medical attention.

By gathering information from both hemispheres, he was able internally to reframe his medical condition. He can be concerned about his healing, and, at the same time, he can also have the internal calm that promotes his healing process.

M: Another example I think is important to share with you involves a client who has been struggling with several physical ailments, one of which is Chronic Fatigue Syndrome.

Prior to working with Internal Dominant Eye Accessing, she could not see an image of herself. She had the sense she was living just above her head and out of her body.

By building an image of herself, beginning with the kinesthetic feeling first, she was able to see an image of herself from the waist up with her right internal eye.

With some practice and patience, she was able to get an image of herself with her left internal eye. The image from her left internal eye was of her from the waist down.

In this example, we built an overall self-image as a hologram, and we brought in the qualities and resources from each internal image into that central holographic image.

With the holographic image, my client could see a complete image of herself from top to bottom.

After we had completed the holographic image, my client reported that she felt much more grounded and in her body.

Finally feeling safe to be in her body was an important piece in my client's healing process.

In our experience, many people diagnosed with Chronic Fatigue Syndrome have, at some point in their lives, had a sense of being disconnected from their bodies. If we are disconnected from our body and its feelings, we may miss important messages about our health. When we are connected to our physical feelings, we are able to receive those important messages from our body before a symptom becomes a serious threat to our health.

A: For our purposes here, it is important to know that building valuable information from both hemispheres into a single perception of self can be the beginning of the healing process.

Once a person has had the experience of being able to access their "other mind's eye," they can easily use their new skill in a variety of contexts.

M: One gentleman I worked with had recently gone back to school to study in the medical field. He was concerned because, even though he spent many hours diligently studying, his test scores were only in the sixty-percent range, which was not high enough to keep him in the program.

He knew he needed to have a more effective way to memorize the names of all the numerous herbs. For all his enthusiasm and efforts, he could not bring his test scores up, and he had developed a fear of taking tests.

The first thing I did was to help him build in a strategy to memorize information using The Hemispheric Eye Memory Strategy. Then he could retrieve the information when he wanted access to it.

Once he had an effective strategy to memorize facts, we then created a compelling self-image of him as a person who has the confidence to comfortably be in a test environment, knowing what he knows.

After two sessions together, my client had practiced his new memory strategy until it became automatic.

Two weeks later my client called to say thank you for the strategy and the self-image. On his very next test he had earned a score of over ninety-percent!

A: Although Marilyn assisted her client in learning an effective strategy to remember facts, and in creating a compelling self-image, it was her client who initiated the proactive behaviors that he had identified in his resource image. Those behaviors allowed him to have the benefits of change.

M: With many of my clients, the resource of being proactive is initially represented in one hemisphere and not the other.

An example of how having the resource of being proactive can make a huge difference involves a client who came to see me at a very low point in his life. He had developed Diabetes in his senior year in high school and was unable to continue playing sports. The shift in his identity eventually led him into a very deep depression. His wife was concerned because she felt that he had no focus in life and was losing the desire to take care of himself.

The Internal Dominant Eye Accessing Process for self-image gave my client a sense of empowerment and control in his life.

One week after our session together, I made a follow-up phone call to see how he was doing. He had gone back to his healthy eating plan and had started to regain some of the weight he had lost. He also had applied to an advanced trade school and was accepted. He now has a focus and a passion for his career, as well as a rekindled interest in other aspects of his life.

A: These are just some of the examples of how people are able to make positive changes in their lives by having conscious access to their fully integrated compelling self-image.

We encourage you to use the processes you have learned here to recognize and utilize your own personal potential. The questions, as well as the answers, are within you. You have more access to both now that you know how to make your unconscious conscious with Internal Dominant Eye Accessing.

Afterword

As is the nature of modern technology, by the time this book was ready to go to press the information available to us has grown dramatically. The basic structure of Internal Dominant Eye Accessing remains solid in it's theory as it is presented in this book, and the applications that apply to understanding and influencing our own internal thinking processes are advancing significantly.

We have discovered many new applications using the basic technology presented in this book. These new advancements give even deeper insights into how we experience life, and how we can take control of our own destiny. The more we learn about *how* our brains code information into emotions, the more precisely we can consciously access the ability within all of us to get the most from all that is possible in the world.

From our experience with participants in workshops and in our private consulting practice, personal changes that consciously incorporate the cognitive style of each hemisphere are complete, and permanent.

It is our commitment to continue our research, and to share our findings in a timely manner through books, tapes, and in seminars. We look forward to connecting with you in the future.

Al & Marilyn Sargent

For information about attending or sponsoring seminars in your area, product information, or consulting, you may contact us by one of the following:

Telephone:	800-807-5666
e-mail:	nlpidea@gte.net
Web site:	www.nlpla.com

Success Design International
P.O. Box 2244
Malibu, CA 90265

Glossary

Accessing Cues

Behaviors that are correlated with the use of a particular representational system; e.g. eye movements, voice tones, postures, breathing, etc. (See Representational Systems)

Amygdala

An almond-shaped structure in the brain that plays a role in emotional coding. It also serves memory function.

Analog

All aspects of communication which are not words including; voice tone, tempo, and body posture.

Analog Marking

Emphasizing a part of a sentence using nonverbal means; e.g. a louder tone or a hand gesture.

Anchor

A cue or trigger that elicits a response, similar to the stimulus-response of classical conditioning.

Associated

Being in an experience or memory as fully and completely as possible (with all the senses); looking out from one's own eyes, hearing from one's own ears, feeling one's own feelings. (See Disassociated, and Dissociated)

Auditory

The sense of hearing. (See Representational Systems)

Backtrack

A spoken or written review or summary of information, usually to build / maintain rapport and to invite revision or correction.

Break State

To change a person's state dramatically. Often used to pull someone out of an unpleasant state.

Behavioral Flexibility

The ability to vary one's behavior in order to elicit a desired response from another person (in contrast to repeating a behavior that hasn't worked).

Calibrate

To "read" another person's verbal and nonverbal responses and associate specific behaviors with specific internal processes or states.

Channel

One of the five senses. (See Representational Systems)

Chunk Size

The size of the object, situation, or experience being considered. This can be altered by chunking up to a more general category, chunking down to a more specific category, or chunking sideways or laterally to others of the same type of class. For example, beginning with "car." you could chunk down to a Ford or to a carburetor, chunk up to a "means of transportation," and chunk sideways to a plane or train.

Collapsing Anchors

See Integrating Response / Anchors.

Complex Equivalence

The complex set of experiences that equal a certain meaning in a person's map of reality; e.g. the specific set of behaviors that indicate that someone loves you.

Congruent

When all of a person's internal strategies, behaviors, and parts are in agreement and working together coherently.

Conscious Mind

The level of experience that is within current awareness, generally recognized as consisting of between five to nine bits of information. Contrast with Unconscious Mind. (See Unconscious Mind)

Contrastive Analysis

Determining the differences between two representations, particularly submodalities.

Context

The environment within which a communication or response occurs. The context is one of the cues that elicit specific responses.

Context Reframing

Placing a "problem" response or behavior in a different context that gives it a new and different—usually more positive—meaning.

Core Transformation®

A process for personal growth that offers a graceful way to change unwanted habits, thoughts, and feelings through discovering a person's "core states."

Corpus Callosum

A network of over 200 million fibers separating the left and right hemispheres of the brain. It transfers information between the left and right hemispheres, allowing the hemispheres to "communicate" with each other.

Criteria

Standards for evaluation; qualities that can be applied to a wide range of specific behaviors or events. Examples: fun, exciting, inexpensive, interesting, high quality, bold, practical, and new.

Critical Submodalities

The submodalitites which are most powerful in determining a person's response. (See Driver)

Disassociated

Being associated into an experience from a perspective outside the aligned position of self, and into another perspective. (See Associated, and Dissociated)

Dissociated

Being disconnected, or separate from, an experience without necessarily changing one's perspective. Without feeling. (See Associated, also Disassociated)

Driver Submodality

The most critical submodality in a given context; changing it automatically changes many other submodalities and "drives" thc response. (Unique for each individual)

Ecology

Considering the effects of a change on the larger system, instead of on just one isolated behavior, part, or person.

Eye Accessing Cues

Movements of a person's eyes that indicate the representational system being used. (See "Accessing Cues)

Firing an Anchor

Repeating the behavior—touch, gesture, voice tone, etc— that triggers a certain response.

First Position ("Self")

Experiencing the world from your own perspective; being fully associated into yourself and your body.

Flexibility

Having more than one behavioral choice in a situation. (See Behavioral Flexibility)

Future Pace

Rehearsing in all systems so that a specific behavior, or set of behaviors, becomes linked and sequenced in response to the appropriate cues and occurs naturally and automatically in future situations.

Guided Search

The process of searching back through one's memories to find experiences that are similar in some way—usually in kinesthetic response. Often used to identify important early formative experiences that continue to affect a person.

Gustatory

Referring to the sense of taste. (See Representational Systems)

Hallucination

An internal representation of, or about, the world that has no basis in present sensory experience.

Hemispheres of the Brain

Referring to halves of the sphere of the brain separated from each other by the Corpus Callosum. (See Corpus Callosum, also Left Hemisphere and Right Hemisphere)

Incongruent

When two or more of a person's representations are in conflict. Being "of two minds." or "torn between two possibilities," etc.

Integrating Responses / Anchors

Eliciting responses simultaneously, in order to blend the experiences.

Installation

Teaching or acquiring a new strategy or behavior, generally by rehearsal or future pacing.

Kinesthetic

The sense of feeling. May be subdivided into tactile feelings (Kt – skin sensing, physically feeling the outside world), proprioceptive feelings (Kp – movement, internal body sensations such as muscle tension or relaxation), and meta feelings (Km – "emotional" responses about some object, situation, or experience). (See Representational Systems)

Lead System

The representational system initially used to access stored information; e.g. making a visual image of a friend in order to get the feeling of liking him / her.

Leading

Guiding another person their ecologically defined outcome.

Left Hemisphere

The left side of the brain. In most people, responsible for the processing of logical, linear information.

Limbic System

A complex, linked set of structures in the brain (including the hippocampus, amygdala, and hypothalamus) thought to be responsible for emotions.

Map of Reality

A person's unique and individual perception of events.

Matching

(See Mirroring, also Pacing)

Meaning Reframing

Ascribing a new meaning to a behavior or response without changing the context. Usually done by directing attention to deleted aspects; e.g. "You thought he was just slow; you didn't notice how thorough and reliable he is."

Meta

Derived from the Greek, meaning beyond or about.

Meta-model

A set of language patterns that focus attention on how people delete, distort, generalize, limit, or specify their realities. It provides a series of questions useful for making communication more specific, recovering lost or unspecified information, and loosening rigid patterns of thinking.

Meta-outcome

The outcome of the outcome: one that is more general and basic than the stated one; e.g. "getting my self-respect back" might be the meta-outcome of "insulting that person."

Meta-person

The observer in an exercise, who has the task of giving sensory feedback to guide (and sometimes also to the person in the "explorer" role) in order to improve performance.

Metaphor

A story, parable, or analogy that relates one situation, experience, or phenomenon to another.

Meta-position

(See Observer)

Milton-model

A set of language patterns useful for communicating directly with the unconscious, influencing and delivering messages in such a way that others readily accept, and respond to, them. Usually vague and, therefore, inclusive language.

Mirroring

Matching one's behavior to that of another person, usually to establish rapport. Sometimes preparatory to leading or intervening. (See Pacing)

Modality

One of the five senses. (See Representational Systems)

Modeling

Analyzing the specific behaviors and thinking patterns of another person or system in order to duplicate their successful results.

Neurological Levels

The logical levels of experience: environment, behavior, capability, belief, identity, and spirit.

Observer Position

A dissociated meta-position from which you can observe or review events, seeing yourself and others interact.

Olfactory

The sense of smell. (See Representational Systems)

Organ Language

Idioms that refer to specific body parts or activities; e.g. "Get off my back," "pain in the neck," etc.

Other Position

To step into someone else's experience or perspective (borrowing a persons perception as a tool for gathering information).

Outcome

Desired goal or result. (See Well-formed Outcome, also Meta-outcome)

Pacing

Matching or mirroring another person's nonverbal and / or verbal behavior. Useful for gaining rapport, sometimes preparatory to leading or intervening. (See Mirroring, also Matching)

Parts

A metaphoric term for different aspects of a person's experience. Parts are distinct from the specific behaviors adopted by the "parts" in order to get their positive outcomes.

Perceptual Filter

An attitude, bias, point of view, perspective, or set of assumptions or presuppositions about an object, person, or situation. This attitude "colors" all perceptions of the object, etc.

Polarity Response

A response which reverses, negates, or takes the opposite position of a previous statement.

Predicates

Process words that express action or relationship with respect to a subject (verbs, adverbs and adjectives). The words may reflect the representational system being used, or they may be non-specific; e.g. "That looks good," "Sounds good to me," "That feels fine," or "I agree".

Preferred Representational System

The representational system which a person habitually uses to process information or experiences; usually the one in which the person can make the most detailed distinctions.

Process Words

(See Predicates)

Rapport

A condition in which responsiveness has been established, often described as feeling safe, trusting, or willing.

Reframing

A process by which a person's perception of a specific event or behavior is altered, resulting in a different response. Usually subdivided into Context Reframing and Meaning Reframing.

Representational System

The internal representations of experience in the five senses: seeing (visual), hearing (auditory), feeling (kinesthetic), tasting (gustatory), and smelling (olfactory).

Resource State

The experience of a useful response. An ability, attitude, behavior, characteristic, perspective, or quality that is useful in some context.

Right Hemisphere

The right side of the brain. In most people, responsible for the processing of spatial awareness and relationship.

Second Position

See Other Position

Secondary Gain

The positive intention or desired outcome (often obscure or unknown) of an undesired or problem behavior.

Self Position

Experiencing the world from your own perspective; being associated into yourself and your body.

Sensory Acuity

The ability to make sensory discriminations to identify distinctions between different states or events.

Sensory Based

Information which is correlated with what has been received by the five senses. (Contrast with Hallucinations)

Separator State

A neutral state between two other states that prevents those states from combining or connecting with each other.

Sorting Polarities

Separating tendencies or "parts" that pull a person in opposite directions into cleanly defined and organized entities. Preparatory to integration.

State

A state of being, or a condition of body / mind response or experience, at a particular moment.

Stealing an Anchor

Identifying a naturally-occurring anchored sequence (stimulus-response) and then firing that anchor--rather than establishing an arbitrary "ad hoc" anchor for the response.

Stimulus-response

The repeated association between an experience and a particular response (Pavlovian conditioning), such that the stimulus becomes a trigger or cue for the response.

Strategy

A sequence of mental and behavioral representations which leads to a specific outcome; e.g. decision, learning, motivation, and specific skills.

Submodalities

The smaller elements within a representational system; e.g. a visual image can be bright, dim, clear, fuzzy, moving, still, large, or small.

Swish

A generative submodalities pattern used to change habits and responses.

Synesthesia

A very close and quick overlap between a sequence of two or more representational systems, such as "see / feel" (feelings ovcrlap with what is seen) or "hear / feel" (feelings overlap with what is heard)

Third Position ("Observer")

A dissociated meta-position from which you can observe or review events, seeing yourself and others interact.

Unconscious Mind

The total experiences and systemic working of the brain, not currently in conscious awareness. (See Conscious Mind)

Visual

The sense of seeing

Well-formed Outcome

A person's goal that is appropriately specified, obtainable, chunked-down, and contextualized, that either helps satisfy, or does not interfere with, the person's other goals.

Bibliography

Dilts, Robert. Tim Hallbom, and Suzi Smith. *Beliefs: Pathways to Health & Well-Being.* **Portland Or: Metamorphous Press, 1993**

Andreas, Connirae and Tamara Andreas. *Core Transformation.* **Moab, Ut: Real People Press, 1994**

Restak, Richard M. *The Brain The Last Frontier.* **New York, NY: Warner Books Inc., 1980**

Restak, Richard M. *The Brain.* **New York, NY. Bantam Books, Inc., 1984**

Restak, Richard M. *The Mind.* **New York, NY. Bantam Books, Inc., 1988**

Calvin, William H., and George A. Ojemann. *Conversations With Neil's Brain.* **Menlo Park, Ca: Addison-Wesley Publishing Company, 1994**

Samuels, Mike M.D., and Nancy Samuels. *Seeing With The Mind's Eye.* **New York, NY. Random House Inc. and The Bookworks, 1988**

Maltz, Maxwell. *Psychocybernetics.* **New York, NY. Pocket Books, A division of Simon & Schuster, 1960**

Appendix

Accessing your internal dominant eye

Step 1: To Demonstrate external eye dominance. (optional)

a) Look at a spot about 20 feet away with your head facing straight.
b) After focusing on the spot simply point at it.
c) Close one eye and notice if your finger is still directly on the spot.
d) Open that eye, then close the other one and notice if your finger is still directly on the spot.
e) The external eye that keeps your finger pointing directly at the spot is your current external dominant eye.
f) Look at the spot again keeping both eyes open and notice that even though you're seeing the object with both external eyes, you're actually seeing it more dominantly with either the left or right eye.
g) This is an external example of what is happening with your internal vision. (your minds eye)
h) A back-up procedure for determining the external dominant eye is noticing which eye you use to look through a camera lens, or a telescope.

Step 2: Get an internal image of a person or of an event.

Step 3: Note the submodalities:

a) Visual
b) Auditory--external and internal
c) Kinesthetics--tactile and proprioceptive
d) Emotional evaluation associated with the image

Step 4: Notice, or simply get a sense of, which internal eye you are seeing that image with.

Step 5: Now in a way that is works for you, shift so that you are now seeing that image with your other internal eye.

Step 6: Note changes in submodalities:
a) Visual
b) Auditory—external and internal
c) Kinesthetics—tactile and proprioceptive
d) Emotional evaluation associated with the image

Hemispheric Specialization of the Brain

Left Hemisphere   **Right Hemisphere**

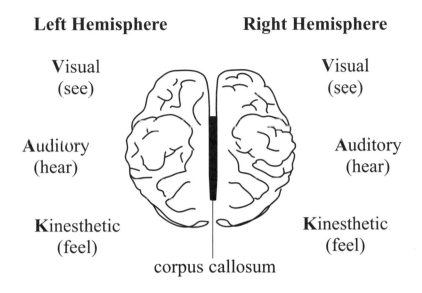

Visual (see)	Visual (see)
Auditory (hear)	Auditory (hear)
Kinesthetic (feel)	Kinesthetic (feel)

corpus callosum

We feel in one world and think and give names in another.

Left Hemisphere	**Right Hemisphere**
Logical	Spatial Information
Linear	Metaphors
Analytical	Sense of Identity
Data	Emotionally Charged Memories
Facts	Total Picture Perceptions
Speech Center	Poetic Language
Familiar Information	Unfamiliar Information

Each hemisphere has an independent capacity for visual, auditory, and kinesthetic processing. Beliefs, strategies, and overall perceptions are unique to the cognitive style of each hemisphere.

CHART A

Visual Pathways

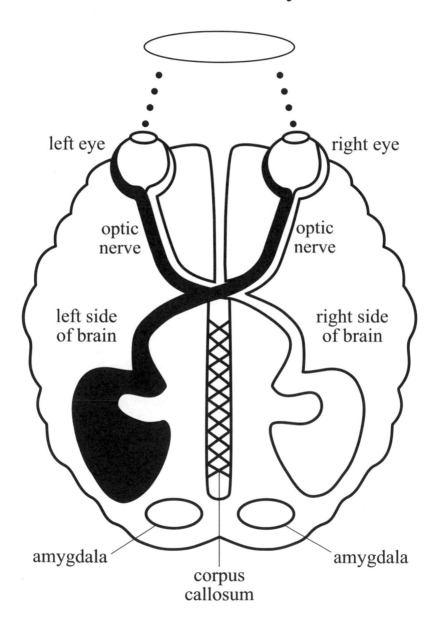

left eye

right eye

optic
nerve

optic
nerve

left side
of brain

right side
of brain

amygdala

amygdala

corpus
callosum

CHART B

Example of Utradian Rhythm
For Hemispheric Dominance

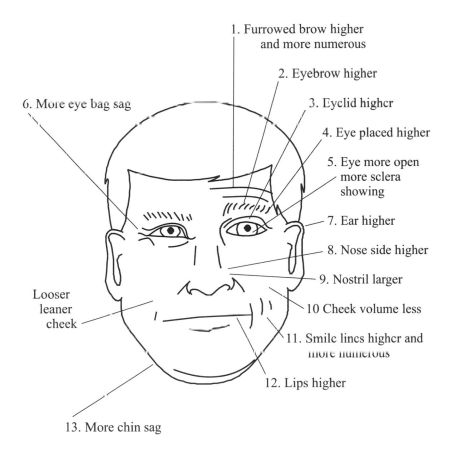

Face lateralization: Left lifted face and mouth line suggesting
right hemispheric dominance at this moment in time.

CHART C

Eye Accessing Cues
Direction of Eye Movement
As You Look At Another Person

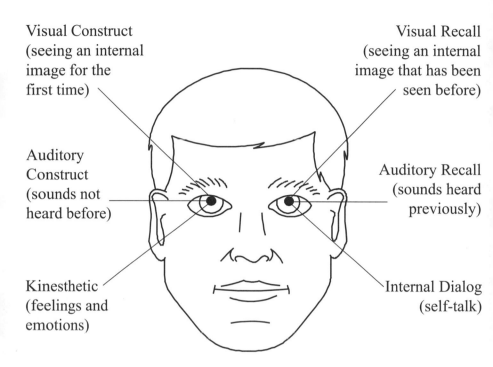

Visual Construct
(seeing an internal
image for the
first time)

Visual Recall
(seeing an internal
image that has been
seen before)

Auditory
Construct
(sounds not
heard before)

Auditory Recall
(sounds heard
previously)

Kinesthetic
(feelings and
emotions)

Internal Dialog
(self-talk)

Over 90% of people are organized this way. This holds true for different cultures and races, as well as male or female. For people who are not organized as shown above, the construct side vertically switches places with the recall side.

To determine how someone is organized, ask two or three questions that require access to visual recall. For a more detailed understanding of eye accessing, contact a Neuro-Linguistic Programming practitioner.

CHART D

The Hemispheric Eye
Foreground-Background Process

Purpose: For the explorer to soften an initial internal response or reaction to a challenging person or situation, while maintaining the ecology necessary for safety.

1: Establish rapport and ecology for working together.

2: Have the explorer think of a challenging person with whom the explorer would like to have a more resourceful initial internal response or reaction. *Example: Supervisor, co-worker, relative, neighbor.*

3: Elicit the explorer's submodalities paying particular attention to:
Visual - Associated or dissociated, clarity, color, movie or still picture, panoramic or framed, size and location.
Auditory - Internal and external voices, volume, location, and content of the words.
Kinesthetic - Tactile, proprioceptive, and emotional evaluation.
Guide calibrates external cues, checking carefully for ecology.

4: Guide says, **"Get a sense of which internal eye you are seeing that image with."** Note response. After response, guide says, **"After checking inside, and in a way that is just right for you, shift your attention to your other internal eye, so that you will be seeing that person now with the information coded in your**

other hemisphere." *Guide notes any change in external cues.*

5:      Elicit any differences in submodalities, paying close attention to any shift in emotional response.

6:      Identify which picture gives the explorer the most choice of responding resourcefully. Have the explorer make this image foreground and leave the less resourceful image background. *Leaving one of the pictures background preserves information and is therefore more ecological.*

7:      Assist the explorer in establishing foreground-background by asking them, **"What would make the resourceful picture stand out?"** Test for response and adjust as appropriate.

8:_   Check to see what follow-up work may be needed. *Doing this process often allows issues to surface, such as limiting beliefs or negatively charged memories. These can then be dealt with using other techniques now, or at a later time.*

9:      Guide tests the explorer's new response by asking, **"When is the next time you will think about, or be with this person, and you want to have your new response?"** Have the explorer imagine being with the person, and calibrate their nonverbal response.

10:      Future pace the new choice the explorer now has to adjust internal dominant eye accessing with this person and with others in the future.

The Hemispheric Eye
Memory Strategy

Purpose: To access left and right hemispheres of the brain to install information and recall for memory.

1. Establish rapport and ecology for working together. Calibrate the explorer for visual memory accessing. (See Chart D in Appendix)

2. Explain and demonstrate explorer's current external dominant eye. *This step shows that there is a difference in eye dominance and will assist in determining the internal dominant eye for The Hemispheric Eye Memory Strategy.*

3. Have the explorer choose a word (noun) that is easy to spell and that he already knows. We will use the example "cat." *This step is to learn the process and to create success.*

4. Have the explorer get a visual image of a cat using his left internal eye, and put this image in his visual recall field. *Usually located up and to the left for visual memory accessing.*

5. Say to the explorer, "Now allow that visual representation of a cat to remain here (*gesture to hold the image in the visual recall field*) as you shift to your right internal eye, and in a way that works for

you, build in the letters 'c-a-t.' Now you are seeing the word 'cat' along with the picture of what a cat looks like."

6.   Next, have the explorer choose a word he would like to be able to spell.

7.   Build a visual representation of what the word means, using the left internal eye. Build the letters for the word with the right internal eye. (*Remember to chunk into small pieces, if needed*).

8.   Repeat Steps 5 & 6 using an image of a person with his telephone number in the image.

9.   Test the explorer's memory of the easy word, the word the explorer chose, and the person with his telephone number.

10.   Discuss with the explorer when and where this process will be useful in his life.

Current Self-Image

Question:

"What is the internal image you currently have of yourself?" or, "When you think of yourself, what do you see?"

Information to gather:

Visual   Size; Location (*gesture to where you see the image*); Color or Black and White; Brightness; Full-body or Part; Posture; Movie or Still; Framed or Panoramic; Height.

_____

_____

Auditory – How does your voice sound?; Tone; Tempo; Volume; What does your voice say? or, What do you say about yourself?

_____

_____

Kinesthetic – How do you feel about yourself? Notice any physical feelings in your body.

_____

_____

Emotions or Evaluations –

_____

_____

Age of the self in the image: _____

Internal eye you are seeing the image with: _____

Creating a Compelling Self-Image
for Specific Behavioral Change

Purpose: To create a self-image that enhances a specific quality or behavior using information from both the left and right hemispheres of the brain.

1.   Establish rapport and ecology for working together, and elicit what quality or behavior the explorer would like to *be different.*

2.   Guide asks, **"What would the you look like that** (*backtrack what the explorer wants to be different*)**?"** *Elicit submodalities and which internal eye the explorer is "seeing" the image with.*

3.   Guide says, **"Now, have a sense of you with this desired quality or behavior with your other internal eye. (Pause) Notice what is different in the second picture."**

4.   Guide says, **"Now that you have access to both pictures, get a sense, or simply notice, which picture is more compelling?"** *(Identify one image as the compelling image and the other as the resource image.)*

5.   Guide asks, **"What information, skill, resource, quality, or feeling is in the resource picture that will enhance and enrich the image of the compelling you?"**

6. Guide says, **"In a way that is just right for you, bring that** (_backtrack resource_) **over now to become a part of the compelling image."**

7. Guide says, **"Notice how having** (_backtrack resource_) **changes the compelling image of you."**

8. Guide asks, **"What other...?"** *(Repeat steps 5, 6, & 7 until all appropriate information has been added to the compelling image.)*

9. Guide has the explorer integrate the compelling self-image into both hemispheres by seeing the compelling image identically through each internal eye.

10. Guide directs the explorer to associate fully into the compelling image by saying: **"Now, I want you to step forward into this compelling image of you. Experience being fully and completely the resourceful you."** Guide says, **"Breathe into the you now that has** (_recap qualities_). **Turn and face the current you, and send a message of encouragement from this compelling you."**

11. Guide has the explorer step back into the current self and receive the message of encouragement from the fully integrated compelling self-image.

12. Test and future pace in several contexts what the explorer will be doing with the new behavior.

Creating a Compelling Self-Image
in Current Reality

Purpose: To create or enhance a congruent and compelling self-image using information from both the left and right hemispheres of the brain.

1.   Establish rapport and ecology for working together

2.   Guide asks, **"When you think of you now, what image do you see?"** *Elicit submodality distinctions and which internal eye the explorer is seeing the image with.* Guide then asks, **"How old are you in this image?"**

3.   Guide says, **"Now in a way that is just right for you, get an image of you with your other internal eye."** *Elicit the differences in submodalities.* Guide then asks, **"How old are you in this image?"**

   Note: If neither image is compelling, or if neither image is of the person, (two images of someone else or two metaphors) have the explorer create a hologram consisting of what they physically look like with some of the positive qualities they know to be true about themselves. If a hologram is required it becomes the compelling image, and the two original images *both* become resource images. If a hologram is used, continue the process with step 5.

4.   Guide says, **"Now that you have access to both images, get a sense, or simply notice, which image is**

more compelling." *Guide allows the explorer to select one image to label as the compelling image and to label the other image as the resource image.*

5. Guide says, **"What information, skills, qualities, resources, or feelings are in the resource image that will enhance and enrich the compelling image?"**

6. Guide says: **"In a way that is just right for you, bring** *(backtrack resource)* **into the compelling image. Notice how having** *(backtrack resource)* **changes the compelling image."**

7. Guide asks, **"What other...?"** Repeat steps 5 & 6 until all appropriate information has been added to the compelling image.

   Note: Not all information needs to be added to the compelling image. Always allow the explorer to determine what information is ecological to add.

8. Guide has the explorer integrate the compelling self-image into both hemispheres by seeing the compelling image identically through each internal eye.

9. Guide directs the explorer to associate fully into the compelling image by saying: **"Now, I want you to step forward into this compelling image of you. Experience being fully and completely the resourceful you. Breathe into the you now that has** *(recap qualities)*. **Turn and face the current you, and send a message of encouragement from this compelling you."**

10. Guide has the explorer step back into current self and receive the message of encouragement from the fully integrated compelling self-image.

11. Guide future paces how the explorer's life will be different with the new self-image, and what new behaviors the explorer will have in the future.
Option: Suggest that the explorer notice this self-image each time the explorer looks in a mirror.

Presuppostitions of NLP

1. *Behind every behavior there is a positive intention.*
    •The person doing a behavior has a positive intention at a deep structure level.
    •When we are changing unwanted behaviors or habits, and moving toward healing, it is necessary to find the deep structure or original intention behind the behavior. We then create new and better choices that preserve the positive intention.

2. *The map is not the territory.*
    •People respond to their map or interpretation of reality, not to reality itself.
    •NLP is about understanding and changing maps, which in turn can change perceptions of reality.

3. *Anything can be accomplished when the task is broken down into small enough chunks.*
    •The goal is "chunked" into pieces that are a manageable size for the individual or system.

4. *There is no such thing as failure, only feedback.*
    •Everything is an learning opportunity to find out what works and what doesn't work.
    •It is important to separate behavior from identity.

5. *People already have all the resources they need.*

•NLP teaches how to access these resources at appropriate times and places.

6.   *Every behavior is useful in some context.*

7.   *If one person can do something, other people can learn from that person's success,*

    •NLP models excellence. It is possible to discover the components and strategies needed to achieve a particular result and to teach it to anyone else.

8.   *The messenger never rests until the message is delivered.*

    •When there is a symptom or communication, it is important to pay attention.

9.   *The meaning of your communication is the response you get.*

    •Communication creates an experience in the listener or reader. The result is the response we elicit. That response may not necessarily match what we intended to communicate.

10.   *Communication is redundant.*

    •We are always sending messages in all three major sensory modalities. NLP checks for congruence in these messages.

11.   *Choice is better than no choice.*

•The element in a system with the most flexibility has the most control.

12. *People always make the best choice available to them at the time.*

    •Often there are better choices. NLP discovers more effective choices and how to create more useful or desirable actions and beliefs.

13. *If what you are doing isn't working, do anything else.*

    •A definition of insanity is doing the same thing over and over again, expecting different results.

Hemispheric Levels of Experience

Left Hemisphere (external)   **Right Hemisphere** (internal)

Mission/Spirit

What do I want to accomplish? *Who or what else is beyond*
What are my goals? *myself?*
What higher connection do I
aspire to?

Identity

What am I? *Who am I?*
How do others describe *What is the deeper sense of*
me? *self only I can experience?*

Beliefs/Values

What things do I believe *What things are important*
to be true? *to me?*
What evidence do I have *What qualities connect to a*
to support my beliefs? *greater purpose?*

Skills/Capabilities

What steps do I take to *What will my physical and*
learn something new? *mental capabilities allow me*
What skills have I learned? *to accomplish?*
What skills do I want to have *What things come naturally*
in the future? *to me?*

Behaviors

What are the behaviors of *What are my behaviors?*
others? *How do my actions influence*
What is happening in the *the environment?*
environment?

Environment

Where and when am I *What is my position in the*
interacting? *environment?*
What facts are verifiable *How does my presence affect*
in the environment? *others in the environment?*

Conditions of a Well-formed Outcome

1. **"What do you want?" (Desired state)**

    a. *Stated in positive terms.* What you *do* want, rather than what you *don't* want.

    b. *Initiated and controlled by client.*

    c. *Specific, sensory-based description of the outcome.* What will the client and others see, hear, and feel when the client has their outcome?

    d. *Appropriate chunk size.* A well-formed outcome is a manageable sized task, appropriate for the client to achieve.

    e. *Meta-outcome:* **"What will having this outcome do for you?"** Verifies that the client will have value from getting their outcome.

2. **"How will you know when you have it?"**

    a. *Appropriate and Timely Feedback.* Sensory based evidence that the client has achieved the desired outcome.

3. **"Where, when, and with whom do you want it?"**

    a. *Is the clients' choice of contexts ecological?* Often, outcomes are ecological in one specific context and not another.

    b. *"Is it sensory-based?"* What specific cues will lead to the new behavior or state?

4. **Ecology. "How will your desired outcome affect other aspects of your life?"** Make sure the desired

outcome has been evaluated for possible negative or positive consequences to other people and other contexts.

5. **"What stops you from having your desired outcome already?"**
   a. *Sensory based description.* Verifiable in current reality.
   b. *Check for meta-model violations.* Language that deletes, distorts, and generalizes: eg: always, never, they, every, etc.

6. **"What resources do you already have that will contribute to getting to your outcome?"** Sensory-based description or demonstration.

7. **"What additional resources do you need to get your outcome?"**

8. **"How are you going to get there?"** (Answer to the best of your ability.)
   a. *Does the client have more than one way to get there?* "How else might you achieve your outcome?" The more alternatives the better.
   b. *Chunking.* Is the first step specified and achievable? Identifying the first step and making sure it is achievable gives the client a roadmap to success that they have control of beginning. Next, identify (chunk) other steps along the way to their outcome.

Submodalitiy Distinctions

Visual
Location
Distance
Associated / Dissociated
Brightness
Foreground / Background
Self / Context
Frequency (multiple images)
Frame / Panorama
Aspect / Ratio (height to width)
Orientation (tilt, spin, etc.)
Density (graininess, pixels)
Transparent / Opaque
Strobe
Direction of lighting
Digital (printing)
Magnification
Texture
3-Dimensional / Flat
Size
Color / Black and white
Saturation (vividness)
Hue or color balance
Shape
Contrast
Focus / horizontal or vertical hold
Sparkle
Perspective (point of view)
Duration
Movement (slide / movie)

Auditory
Location
Tone
Tempo
Volume
Rhythm
Continuous / Interrupted
Timbre
Digital (words)
Associated / Dissociated
Duration
Number (voices / sounds)
Symmetry
Resonance with context
External-Internal (source)
Monaural / Stereo
Distance
Contrast
Figure-ground
Clarity

Kinesthetic
Pressure
Location
Extent
Texture
Temperature
Number
Symmetry
External-Internal (source)